HOMES AND HOUSES

OF HEREFORDSHIRE

Frontispiece: The Rodd (from a painting by Mary Rennell)

HOMES AND HOUSES OF HEREFORDSHIRE

by
MARY ANDERE

with a Foreword by Roy Strong

EXPRESS LOGIC: HEREFORD

Express Logic Ltd
Foley Estate, Hereford, HR1 2SJ

TO

Marjorie and Jim Hunnisette

'Finally, brethren, whatsoever things are true, whatsoever things are honest, whatsoever things are just, whatsoever things are pure, whatsoever things are lovely, whatsoever things are of good report; if there be any virtue, and if there be any praise, think on these things.'

Philippians 4:8

First published 1977

British Library Cataloguing in Publication Data

Andere, Mary
Homes and Houses of Herefordshire.
1. Herefordshire – Social life and customs
I. Title
942.4'4 DA670.H4

ISBN 0-904464-10-5

Also by Mary Andere

Herefordshire The Enchanted Land
Old Needlework Boxes and Tools
Thomas Traherne: The Image and Other Selections

Printed in Great Britain by
Print Logic Ltd, Hereford

CONTENTS

FOREWORD

Herefordshire has never been a county for the grandest of houses. Too far from London until the advent of the railways, the great of court and government raised their mansions in the home counties or fashionable Northamptonshire. It was not in fact until the second half of the seventeenth century that the county families began to express themselves in country houses of importance, the Scudamores at Holme Lacy, the Foleys at Stoke Edith, the Batemans at Shobdon or the Coningsbys at Hampton Court. But it was only at the close of the eighteenth century that Herefordshire was to make its own unique contribution to the art of the English country house in Sir Uvedale Price's Foxley and Richard Payne Knight's Downton. Both these houses, together with their landscaped environs, were bold and uncompromising statements of a revolutionary aesthetic which was to sweep away the ordered symmetrical world of Adam, Chambers and Capability Brown, the Picturesque. This, with its cult of the assymetrical, the rambling and romantic, its delight in mystery and surprise, changed the course of English country house architecture and gardening. And the fount of all this was these two Herefordshire country gentlemen.

Sadly most of these great houses have long since vanished in a terrible roll call of destruction which begins with Urishay Castle in 1921. How sad to think that Sir Samuel Rush Meyrick's Goodrich Court was swept away by the bulldozer, its glories reduced to rubble sold at half a crown a ton! Although Garnons still magnificently commands its great Repton landscape, two thirds of the house has gone forever. There can be no more poignant record of a vanished house than the book recording the Hoskyns family of Harewood Park laid in the side chapel at Abbey Dore. The great house was destroyed as target practice in 1952 and all that now remains is a ruined stable block and the shafts of noble columns cast to the ground. Close by an inscription on an arch to the abandoned church records the generations of Hoskyns who have passed that way to pray and to the grave.

Changes in the structure of our society have rendered such buildings obsolete. The great house now has no future save as a multiple living unit, a tourist attraction or adapted to some alternative use. Croft Castle and Berrington Hall belong to the National Trust, Holme Lacy is now a hospital. Others, still in the hands of descendants of their builders, fling open their gates to the public: gloomy, compelling Eastnor Castle, romantic Kentchurch or eccentric Dinmore.

When one thinks of homes it is not these which spring to mind anymore but the lesser manor houses, the farm houses, rectories and vicarages which lie scattered all over the county. These alone still have a future as houses to live in because most have a basis in a working reality. This is crucial and gives the impetus and drive which has ensured their restoration and conservation. But the past has its dangers. It can eat the present and eliminate the will to a future.

Conservation can destroy our ability to go on creating. In the past to build a house in the country epitomised success and a faith in what was to follow. Today, in the absence of optimism, we prefer to restore and re-create within the past. Such an attitude has guaranteed that our heritage of medium sized historic houses is assured but, as a consequence, it has eliminated any hope of a contemporary heritage of twentieth century Herefordshire houses and homes to bequeath to our descendants.

March 1977 Roy Strong

PREFACE

In a book of this size it would be impossible to include all the houses in Herefordshire which have particular features of interest, beauty, legend, or other claims to distinction; and no one is more aware of this than the writer. Nor would it have been right and proper to try to differentiate between this house and that, in what would have been an almost impossible task. The final result therefore has of necessity had to be not a selection, but almost a short catalogue, solely of those houses which it was possible to visit within the space of time available. It has been suggested that the many houses omitted could perhaps form the basis for another volume, and this is always a possibility for those areas of the county which had to be left out of this volume.

I would also add that some owners have preferred not to be included, since past publicity has left their homes liable to invasion from those who refused to respect their privacy. It is sincerely to be hoped that no reader of this book will display any such lack of courtesy, but in order that there may be no confusion in the matter, an appendix is included giving details of those houses which are open to the public, and also an indication of opening times and arrangements.

Local historians and other specialists may feel that there is much omitted which they would have added had they been writing this book. This is a deliberate intention, partly because this is not a book for the specialist, but for the general reader, for those who wish to tour the county either by car, or from an armchair, without becoming too involved in technical details; and partly also because there are already so many excellent booklets written on most areas by local historians. The work which has been put into that kind of study is of a specialised nature, and I personally would wish that such leaflets were more easily available in village shops, churches and other places in each area, since they add greatly to the interest for those who have the time and wish to delve more deeply into history. As such, this present book offers no form of competition, though it is hoped that it may perhaps stimulate an interest which can then be furthered by such booklets.

Apart from fiction, few books are really the work of one person. For the most part I have had to depend very largely on the help and goodwill of a very large body of people who have assisted the work of research by one means or another, and have made available personal records and memories in the most generous ways. One by-product in the gathering of material for this book is an awareness both of the extraordinary kindness and helpfulness buried, like a treasure, deep in the majority of mankind, and of the number of homes in England where happiness still reigns almost tangibly, regardless of the depressing stories appearing daily in the national press of unhappy, tragic homes. These two factors in themselves have made the work on this book a real pleasure.

Amongst those whom I would particularly wish to thank for their help and kindness in this matter are: Mrs R. Aldrich-Blake; Mr Frank Amos, and Mr Harry Amos; Mr A. H. Bailey; Sir Deryk Bailey; Mr M. F. Borrill; Mrs Ann Carter; Mr J. P. F. Clay; Lord Croft of Croft Castle; Mr and Mrs Bernard Curtis; Mr J. H. Davies; Miss M. Evans; Miss Rose Farr-Smith; Mr and Mrs Richard Gaskell; the late Mrs F. Gaze; Mr and Mrs Gittoes; Mrs Doris E. Griffiths; Mr and Mrs Christopher Harley; Maj. and Mrs R. C. Hereford; the Editor of the *Hereford Times*; Mr Frank Hoddell; Mr and Mrs John Hoddell; the Revd and Mrs John Hoskyns; Miss Jenny Houston; Mrs A. Jenkins; Mr Colin Jones; Mr and Mrs William Jones; Mr and Mrs E. R. Jordan; Mr and Mrs Stephen Joyce; Mr and Mrs Victor Keegan; Mr and Mrs D. J. Lee; Mr and Mrs B. Lewis; Mr and Mrs Clive D. Lindley; Mr and Mrs Joseph Lloyd; Mr H. Lynch-Blosse; Mr and Mrs Robin Malim; the late Mr Ian Murray and Mr John Murray; Sir Humphrey and Lady Mynors; Miss Ruth Sagar of the National Trust; Miss P. J. A. Owen; Mrs Derek Powell; Mr and Mrs Derek Preece; Mrs S. Preece; Mr and Mrs W. A. Price; Lord and Lady Rennell of Rodd; Mr and Mrs Kim Richardson; Mr D. Saunders; Mrs G. Saunders; the late Lt-Cdr Lucas-Scudamore and the Lady Patricia Lucas-Scudamore; Lt-Cdr and Mrs Robert Simpson; Mr and Mrs Colin Shepherd; Mr and Mrs D. Taborn; Mr John Trafford; Miss Mary Vaughan; Mrs M. Walsh; Mr and Mrs Claude Waters.

To these I must add especial thanks and gratitude for the tireless endeavours of the Staff of the Hereford City Library, the Hereford County Library, and the Ross Library, who have responded so valiantly to the many and varied enquiries with which I constantly presented them for research purposes. I am greatly indebted also to Lynnette Chamberlain, and to Peter Manders, for their kindness in allowing me to use their illustrations; to Mary Rennell, who so kindly offered to do a painting of The Rodd which I could use in this book (a second illustration of The Rodd may be seen in *The Paintings and Drawings of Mary Rennell*); to the Editor of *Country Life* for permission to use certain photographs; and to Mr John Bullough, who took so many of the photographs I needed – and not when the summer suns were glowing, but all too often, because of the exigencies of time, when snow had been falling, winds and rain were blowing, and winter skies made for difficulties of light and shade. I owe a special and very personal debt to Miss Helen B. Ward, who gave up her time to act as chauffeur on occasions when I would not have been able to drive myself; and to Mrs E. Rudge, without whose help in a dozen different directions in the home the actual effort of collating the material would never have been sustained.

In conclusion, I especially appreciate the kindness of Dr Roy Strong in sparing the time to read the manuscript and write the Foreword to this book.

Ross-on-Wye
March 1977

Mary Andere

LUDLOW
A 4113
Brampton Bryan
LUDLOW
SHREWSBURY
A 456
KIDDERMINSTER
BIRMINGHAM
KIDDERMINSTER
B4203
A 4110
Croft Castle
A 49
Eardisland
A 44
LEOMINSTER
Pembridge
A 44
A 4112
A 44
Brockhampton
A 44
WORCESTER
BROMYARD
A 4111
Weobley
A 4112
Kings Pyon
A 4110
WORCESTER
Black Mountains
Eardisley
Whitney
A 438
Mansel Lacy
Huntington
Burghill
A 465
Cradley
A 4103
A 4105
RIVER WYE
A 438
A 49
Tyberton
Bosbury
EVESHAM
A 449
Hereford Beacon
B 4348
B 4352
HEREFORD
B 4224
Hampton Bishop
LEDBURY
A 438
TEWKESBUR
Madley
Eastnor
B 4348
B 4399
A 49
Vowchurch
Fownhope
A 417
GLOUCESTER
A 449
A 465
Abbey Dore
Kilpeck
B 4348
Hoarwithy
RIVER WYE
M 50
Clodock
Pontrilas
ROSS·ON·WYE
A 40
A 40
GLOUCESTER
0
5
SCALE
ABERGAVENNY
Goodrich
Whitchurch

Chapter 1

LIFE STYLES AND HOUSE STYLES

THE title of this book may sound like a tautology. But if the words are examined there is a distinction. Man has not always lived in a house, but from the earliest times he has had a home, of whatever type. The *Concise Oxford Dictionary* defines the words as: 'House: building for human habitation.' 'Home', on the other hand, is 'a dwelling-place, fixed residence of family or household.' Strictly, therefore, a house is a man-made construction of some sort of material brought to the spot; whereas a home can be in a cave or a hole in the ground, or in any place where men live in community as a family or larger group and where, as the definition continues, 'one feels at ease'. Normally, and fortunately, the two coincide and a house is also a home, though there are always sad cases where this is not necessarily so.

In early times it was necessary to use those materials most readily available in the construction of a house. Labour may have been plentiful, since in the old tribal communities all were called upon to help, including women and young children; but transport over any great distance had its problems. Consequently, for many centuries, the ordinary man's house was built of local materials, and according to the skill or manpower available.

Today we are learning more than has been known for centuries about our early forebears, with archaeologists finding remains of buildings, tools, burials, and other things which speak to them more authentically than ever words can do. In the last fifty years or so our knowledge of history has been radically changed and enlarged in all areas.

Herefordshire is particularly rich in the number of hill-forts, or hill-encampments, which bear evidence of early British origins. We know now that here they lived in rectangular-shaped, single-roomed, timber-framed houses, with roofs made either of skins or of straw. These are probably the direct ancestors of Herefordshire's present timber-framed houses. In other areas, where there were many swamps and lakes, men built wood and wattle houses in the lakes on great wooden piles, and in the northern parts of Britain the houses were often round and made of stone.

With the coming of the Romans a certain amount of the new culture and civilization was taken over. It was Roman policy to encourage inhabitants of occupied countries to forsake their former villages and live in the townships erected for them by their conquerors. They knew that people who accept an urbanised type of life are easier to handle, becoming addicted to material comforts, and less likely to retain tribal links and hatred of the conquerors. But neither the Roman nor the Romano-British towns in Britain contained anything like the architectural glories associated in our minds with Rome and other great cities of the Mediterranean Empire. The buildings in Britain, even in towns such as Colchester, Winchester, Verulamium, Silchester and others, were on a far less grandiose scale; and climatic conditions had a certain amount to do with this. One of the best books for descriptions and drawings of the Roman way of life in Britain is *Britain in the Roman Empire*, by Prof. J. Liversidge, and some of the newest ideas about Roman towns are to be found in Prof. G. C. Boon's book, *Silchester, the Roman Town of Calleva.* We realise that apart from the official administrative buildings, temples, baths, barracks and so on, the average dwelling was mostly of timber framework, with lath and plaster or sometimes rough brickwork infilling.

There are remains of Roman villas in Herefordshire, but so far only comparatively few have been found, due mainly to the difficulties of finance where archaeological exploration is concerned. Usually they were owned by Romans or Romano-Britons. A large villa could have as many as thirty or forty rooms, often on two storeys; and was built around a large open courtyard with the chief rooms on the north and eastern sides, and the western side holding the kitchens, larders and various storerooms. The fourth side of the square was normally a plain wall with a large gateway in the centre, sometimes surmounted by a watch-tower. A covered corridor, or veranda, ran around the three sides of the court; and nearly all villas had a hypocaust form of central-heating so that rooms were warm and comfortable and there was a good supply of hot water for the kitchens and baths – essential in any form of Roman society.

Work in the villa and on the surrounding land was undertaken by a staff of labourers and slaves. An efficiently run household would be a self-contained unit which could support itself in nearly all important matters. Wheat and vegetables were grown, animals kept, so food was seldom scarce. On the staff would be a carpenter, a potter and other artisans, and most households wove their own materials. Apart from such things as glass or especially fine metalware, or ornaments and other non-essentials, there was seldom need to depend on the towns for supplies. Slaves were valuable possessions, for which the owner had often paid a good deal, and as such it was in his own interest that they should be well-fed, healthy and fit enough to work well. Compared with that of the simple village peasants, who had to pay taxes, face crop-failures and generally depend on their own individual efforts, the life of a slave was seldom too terrible. A good slave, with a good master, was almost one of the family; he need not worry about his shelter, clothing or meals, and knew he was secure for life.

With the recall of the Roman Army *c.* 410, life in the old, pleasant style of the Roman civilization broke down. The Dark Age meant that men left the towns and villages wherever possible and congregated on the hilltops where the old British camps had been. The local headman, or prince, seems to have built his hall there, refortified the circumference of the camp and made the whole into a stronghold where all lived together in a communal way of life. When danger threatened, all joined in defence, and all able-bodied males went out to attack. People lived, therefore, within the security of a close-knit community, bound by ties either of blood or of mutual dependence. No one was overworked, but equally no one was allowed to shirk. Daily life was lived within the confines of the large hall, where meals were taken and where all slept. Stores, workshops, stables, outhouses, animal pens, were outside the hall but within the perimeter protective barricade. Guards were posted on look-out duty, so that all within the camp could rest secure and have no need to keep perpetual watchfulness on their own account. Despite all the perils of the times, human and animal foes, wind, weather, pestilence and other ills, the inmates of these Dark Age forts probably had far less sense of pressure, and knew more feeling of security, than many people in our more isolated way of living today.

Once the invading hordes of Saxons had settled on the land, forsaking their role as pirates and brigands seeking territory, they too formed their own way of life, on the lines they had known it in Northern Holland and Schleswick. It was a different way of life from the old Romano-British way, founded on other laws and loyalties.

In Anglo-Saxon England society was based entirely on the tie of blood. Each class, tribe or family lived by itself, forming itself into a group for mutual protection. The death of any one member by violence was an obligation on his kinsmen to avenge the murder by feud. Equally, the clan as a whole was answerable for the ill-deeds of any of its own members. The small, individualised villages were usually surrounded by rough stockades or thorn hedges, and the only houses of which we have much knowledge are those of the nobles, or the headman of each village. The hovels of the churls were probably of a most primitive type. But the headman's hall consisted of one large, long room which formed the eating, sleeping and living quarters. Sleeping benches, used by day as shelves, were against the walls, and along the length of the hall were tables with benches and stools. In the centre was a long hearth, giving not only heat, but light, and the smoke curled upwards to a hole in the high roof above. At the end of the hall was a dais for the chief and his family, with table and chairs. Here, also, was the gift-stool, where after a foray each member of the band had his portion of the spoils handed out to him. Old illuminations show that cooking was done out of doors, probably for safety reasons, and must have been a never-ending task with whole oxen being boiled in immense cauldrons or roasted over huge fires. The Saxons had little use for learning or culture; food, females and folk-songs were their delight in life, spiced always with fighting, either against an enemy or amongst themselves, for the sheer joy of physical prowess.

So far only a small proportion of the population could be said to have houses of their own. Life continued in a fairly even tenor during the years of the Anglo-Saxon kings, though from the Bayeux tapestries worked by the Norman ladies we know that there were improvements in the Anglo-Saxon hall by the end of the 10th-11th centuries. One scene depicts Harold feasting with his friends in a stone-built, no longer timbered, style of house, two-storeyed, with the hall raised over the vaulted ground floor (used for storage purposes), and with an external staircase leading to the upper floor. The rounded arches of the room below indicate that Norman fashions in architecture were already influencing building in England before the Conquest, and superseding the Saxon hall described previously. In Lincolnshire, at Boothby Pagnell, there is an excellent example of this type of building, and Herefordshire is fortunate in having a similar example remaining at Brinsop Manor. In this type of hall the fireplace was always placed in the wall, with a cylindrical chimney above it, eventually adorned by the great fireplace hoods which form so magnificent a framing for these hearths. The old, single-floored, wooden hall still had its central hearth, but the manner of life lived within both types was much the same, a communal form of life still with the lord and his family having the privileged platform of the dais, but the rest of the household eating, sleeping and living in the one great room.

But by the 13th century England had begun to develop what we now recognise as an essentially English way of life. Buildings, customs, habits, now had distinctive national traits and Norman and Saxon cultures were becoming firmly welded into one national unity. This was the time when the basis of our present parliamentary system was laid down – oddly enough by the lords, or barons, ensuring for the commoners that they should have their own representatives in Parliament, thus forming the foundation of what we know as the Lower House. It is interesting to realise that it was in fact the Lords, or Upper House, who first upheld the liberty of the people and insisted on a democratic form of government, and not the other way round.

Now serfs began to be able to buy their freedom, and often migrated to the towns. Others merely decided to pay rent for their land, instead of giving service as previously. The more peaceful conditions of the country meant that foreign service was not now likely to drain manpower from the land as before, and the strong hand of Edward I ensured that there was little opportunity for in-fighting amongst his subjects. Castles and manors could therefore begin to expand a little. As more fully described in *Herefordshire, The Enchanted Land,* until the Normans came to Britain private strongholds, or castles, had been unknown. But after the Conquest, and more particularly in the reigns of Henry I and Stephen, great square, or round, stone keeps began to be erected, the sort of buildings to which the Norman barons had been accustomed in their native land but which were alien to the Anglo-Saxon way of life. Now, however, a castle no longer needed to be a fortress composed mainly of mass, with narrow windows and a minimum of exits. Plans for improvements in living conditions could thus be entertained. A chapel now became sited in the castle yard rather than in the castle itself, and butteries, kitchens and living quarters could be built there also. Windows could become larger, and the halls of the barons began also to take on a lighter, more airy look.

Then, in 1349, the Black Death intervened with traumatic effects, breaking up what was becoming a strong, peaceful and prosperous country. It claimed about one third of the population, having no regard for status, age or wealth. The Hundred Years War, which had begun in 1338, finished off the old system for ever since, combined, the two calamities led to such a rise in prices, and such a scarcity of labour, that discontent and the equivalent of modern bankruptcy were widespread; something akin to our Demos began to be known. The serfs, as a class, disappeared for ever, and feudalism and its way of life was on the way out. In the towns the merchant guilds protected the rights of the wealthier citizens. In retaliation the craftsmen and artisans began to form the craft guilds to protect their interests. Trade unions are not new by any manner of means.

During the 14th century the manor house, still often fortified by a moat, began to take the place of the castle for the lower ranks of aristocracy. These manors consisted mainly of the great-hall, lineal descendant of the old halls of the Dark Age and the Anglo-Saxon era, and hardly different. The lord and his family had continued living on the dais, taking their meals there and receiving guests; but now were added the two side-wings containing the solar, beyond the dais and on an upper floor, and the buttery and pantry at the other end, divided off from the hall behind a screen. The screens had originally been separate, moveable ones, set by the doors to prevent draughts blowing smoke from the fire all round the hall. Now they became a continuous structure, usually of wood, but pierced with two doors leading from the hall into what now is known as the screens passage. The manner of life was still communal, but the lord and his lady now had some form of privacy in their private quarters in the solar wing. The word derives from the Old French *soler,* or an upstairs room, which itself stemmed from the Latin meaning a sunning-place, or sun-room.

In the following century the roof construction of these great-halls became more elaborate, with certain distinctive features. There is a wealth of books dealing with the subject and a number of these are included in the List of Sources. The walls of these halls were usually covered with some form of decoration, either tapestry or cloth, though in the simpler ones it was more often plaster and boarding, with war and hunting trophies and weapons added for local colour. Beams and walls alike were sometimes stained or painted with simple geometric designs.

But, as the Herefordshire poet William Langland complains so bitterly in his fourteenth-century *Vision of Piers Plowman,* now the rich 'have a rule to eat by themselves in a privy parlour . . . and leave the chief hall That was made for meals, for men to eat in . . . '

By Tudor times the original simplicity of the medieval mode of living was becoming lost under more complex forms. Now 'servants knew their place' – which was to keep to the kitchens and be less visible about the rooms for the family. The original great-hall and its two wings began to throw out further wings. From now on, through Elizabethan and Jacobean eras, the ground plan began to take on new forms. The plain straight line gradually became an *E*, with extended wings and a central porch added in front of the main door of the old-style hall. Later the *E* developed into an *H* as rooms were added on to either wing at the back. Rooms serving different purposes became common, and more privacy still was possible for the wealthier members of society. By the time of Henry VIII brick was more fashionable than stone, and many of the mansions now being constructed used it and thus developed new architectural styles. The houses of the simple gentry were less ostentatious, still frequently being timber-framed, with lath-and-plaster or brick infilling. But in the larger houses more rooms made corridors a necessity; buildings gradually became rambling, as extensions were added and open spaces roofed over, often in a somewhat haphazard manner, to allow easier and warmer access from place to place. Ceilings began to be plastered, painted, panelled or beamed, according to the size of the house and taste of the owner. Walls were panelled and carved, and furniture became a feature with decorative intent instead of plain utility.

But it was not until Elizabethan times that the great-hall's position was finally altered. Then, instead of forming the main frontage of the house, it was placed centrally, at right angles to the entrance, thus becoming virtually an entrance-hall, though still one of vast proportions in the larger mansions. Its original need to serve as a communal living-room no longer existed. There were rooms in plenty now for living in. The wealthy members of society began to revel in the freedom which their own (often newly-acquired) social status gave them; and parlours, great chambers, ante-rooms, and long galleries 'where gentle exercise might be taken', began to proliferate. True, on special occasions banquets could still take place in the hall, but for the most part the family ate in the new-fangled dining-rooms. The disintegration of the old communal way of life and the easy, familiar ties between the lord and his retainers gradually became more fully formalised, with sharp divisions being at last clear-cut. Retainers became servants relegated to their own quarters usually centring on the kitchen regions.

By now the homes of the middle classes were very comfortable, with panelled walls and timbered or plastered ceilings. Carpets were becoming more common instead of the rushes which had strewn the floors of old. Possessions began to accrue. Pewter utensils were common; silver began to show its face, modestly at first, in the homes of the middle classes. Wills of the period frequently mention, as being especially regarded and of some value, such items as 'my silver spoon' or even 'the silver thimble that my father gave me'. Some of the old traditional Tudor-style houses with their patterned timbering and white plaster panels began to be rebuilt in brick, or sometimes were merely encased in it, in humble imitation of the more ornate Italianate brick mansions of the really wealthy.

By the late 17th century the Classic influence had completely altered the form of the house. New social conditions had also played their part in this change. Squarish in design, the hall now shrank to a mere hall-way in which guests could be received and then siphoned off into the main rooms on either side, or led via the staircase to the upper floor. A living-room (parlour still in country districts), a dining-room, and a library were important evidence of social standing, gradually increasing again and developing into the need for a morning-room, or breakfast-room, with ante-rooms, smoking-rooms, music-rooms and whatever else fashion or taste might dictate. Roofs were nearly always of slate, stone or tiling, frequently hipped instead of simply gabled, following the Continental styles now so widely known and admired.

In Herefordshire there are none of the huge, palatial mansions such as Hampton Court at Richmond, Knowle Park in Kent, East Bursham Manor in Norfolk, or Sutton Place in Surrey. It was by now too remote from the corridors of power for the nobles and aristocrats to spend their time in its soft green paradise. Its great days were nearly past, when kings had known and loved its hills and valleys, and when its bishops and barons had counted for so much in the making of England's history. But it was rich in the type of houses which were built for the lesser nobility and for the wealthy citizen or landowner. In the ensuing centuries, when money came into its own and began to be of more importance than mere land in the economic life of the country, men moved up or were pushed down the social scale with greater fluidity than ever; and the first thing a man did on rising higher was, as through all centuries, to buy or build himself a house. It is interesting to note that in Herefordshire many of the houses still retain clear indications of the old medieval structure, even though they were built centuries later. Fashion always moves slowly, and the further the distance from the hub of a country the longer it takes for ideas to filter through and become accepted. Frequently, therefore, architecture in the more remote counties such as Cornwall, the border counties, Shropshire and the far North, is fifty to a hundred years behind the latest styles in London and the fashionable areas. Thus the main door still often opened directly into the hall, now re-christened the dining-room, but the true descendant of the old-style hall, with the doors to the parlour, or withdrawing-room, still opening off at one end of the longer room, near the main door, just as once the solar had opened off the hall.

During the 18th century the conditions and ways of life were changed completely for nearly all the population by such a simple yet far-reaching innovation as the introduction of the turnip for the winter-feeding of cattle. Through such homely discoveries are the paths of history irrevocably altered for mankind. Now cattle could be kept alive throughout the winter, thus continuing to yield milk and making for the availability of fresh meat all year round instead of the old, often slightly unpalatable, salted meat. Now, instead of leaving fields fallow for one year in three, as had been the custom from time immemorial, turnips were grown on them in the fallow year. This meant that when cattle were turned on to them to graze, the soil was manured and so became more prolific for the next crop. The four-course system of crop-rotation was introduced, as well as selective breeding of cattle. England, once famous for its sheep and wool-trade, now took the lead in live-stock farming and new methods of agriculture.

But from the mid 18th century, alongside the increased wealth gained by the new farming methods, almost unnoticed in England under the shadow of the French Revolution, was rising the equally sinister Industrial Revolution. Had the French troubles not distracted the nation's attention from its own affairs, the results of the Industrial Revolution might have been less disastrous, and less damaging to the social structure of the country. Progress for the working man and his conditions might well have gone hand-in-hand with mechanization and industrial progress. As it was, fear of uprisings, fear of the mob, fear by every man for every man outside his own immediate circle, made for a rigidity in the social structure which was a hindrance to all true progress. It laid also the foundations for the bitter antagonism which was to arise between the capitalist-industrialist and the working class, which remains to our own day. The old, responsible relationship of the landowner, whose family had often grown up through centuries alongside the families of tenants and workers, was badly undermined by a variety of events. The General Land Enclosure Act of 1801 was an attempt to counteract the effects of the Napoleonic blockade which almost succeeded in bringing England to the verge of starvation. The Act meant that small-holdings and common lands were attached to large farms in an attempt to ensure essential large-scale production of wheat. (The communal farms of the Soviet Union are an attempt to solve this problem in much the same manner, but under Socialist theory; and they seem just as conspicuously unpopular with the labourers and even less successful productively.) Once deprived of their own few acres, however meagre, men tended to drift into the towns to find employment. This played into the hands of the industrialists who had a vast labour market from which to pick and choose and who could hold the threat of unemployment over the heads of the rebellious. It also meant a great increase in the need for housing and speculators were as common then as now. Human nature does not change, though the optimist deludes himself. The row upon row of uninspired and uninspiring tenements which blossomed were possibly better and more attractive in their prime than they look today, but the conditions of life within them, often with several families living in one house, left a great deal to be desired. And the long rows of terraced houses in the industrial North made no pretence at all to either architectural or social merit. Yet even these may have imparted a greater sense of community and security than the high-rise flats which were to be so peculiar a feature of the 20th century.

During the 19th century the conditions of life of the lower classes became so appalling as to excite the compassion and indignation of many of the reformers of the day, whose consciences had been roused by the evangelical revival stemming from Wesley's preaching at the end of the 18th century. Once the conditions of work in the factories and mines, and the squalor in which many workers were housed became known, it was the oft-maligned Victorians who, through their religious groups, writers and sociologists, began to press for improvements. They succeeded, long before Marx became so vociferous, in bringing about a series of Acts connected with education, health and factory conditions. It is all too often unrecognised that it was the Victorians themselves who wrestled with the problems which they had inherited. They succeeded in righting so many of the wrongs and inherent evils left them that their era became one of the most prosperous ever known by the majority of the inhabitants of this island. However poor many of the poorest were, they were still infinitely better legislated for than had been their ancestors of the previous century; and in terms of finance most of them were far better provided for than their forebears. By the Edwardian era many of the greatest evils had been tackled or were being dealt with further, and the unhappy incident of history known to us as the Great War, like the Black Death so long before, dealt a traumatic blow to society from which it has never been able to recover.

But now, in the approaches to the 20th century, more and more people possessed their own houses, either purchased or rented. The Victorian style suburban house was ubiquitous, with its squarish rooms, narrow hallway, and kitchen and scullery at the back. For large numbers of people all over England this was now the standard type of house – very far removed from their ancestors' manner of life not so many years before. Now each family tended to live in its own small, private 'castle', many of them still served by one or more domestics even in the lowest social grades, and often sheltering elderly parents or unmarried aunts and uncles or other relatives within the family bosom.

But the fashion gradually grew that upon marriage each couple should seek its own house, or at least its own apartments, however humble. So far as living-in domestics were concerned, the hey-day was over, and in the ensuing years, right down to our own time, they would become a greater and greater rarity. Unlike the Dodo, which 'could fly, but wouldn't', they could and did. The practice of each couple seeking its own private nest also incidentally hastened the break-up of the last vestigial remnants of the old communal life and, finally, of the close-knit family ties. As houses became smaller and more box-like, and as the demands of Empire and the new, commercial-type companies caused employees to move from one town to another, or from one country to the far side of the world, so the family pattern had to be shed. In the 20th century the last link with the old ways of life has finally been broken for most families.

In Herefordshire, with its lack of industrial life, things still moved in the old-fashioned, leisurely style. But because transport, both internally and internationally, had so much improved, the nation was no longer dependent on its home-produced corn and cattle and the lot of the agricultural community tended to decline. The landed classes still lived in comparative comfort, but more and more, through to our own day, the drift of the farm-worker to the towns continued. The social structure changed once again. What had become 'the staff', instead of 'the servants', became eventually a non-existent staff so far as the busy mistress of a house was concerned. Her job of knowing how to direct her domestics, knowing exactly how each task should be done, how long it should take and what is involved in it, but never expecting to engage in it herself except in emergencies, has undergone a different sort of revolution. Now she is indeed and in truth 'the busy housewife' who, with the doubtful blessing of mechanical aids galore, has all too often to tackle all jobs, inside and outside the house, on her own or with the minimum of daily help, let alone being transport driver-in-chief for the family, and frequently mechanic and electrician as well. It is perhaps all the more to her honour that in all my travels researching for this book I was constantly struck by the pleasantness and orderliness of the many homes I visited, by the sense of love and warmth generated in them, and by the obvious pride which shone through from both the furnishings and décor.

The sense is still deeply ingrained in English men and women that, though beleaguered by many foes their ancestors never knew – foes of finances, extortionate taxes and rates, domestic anxieties and continual national crises – yet still the English home is the Englishman's castle. On it, and in it, he expends his love and energy, creating within its walls that sense of home which, intangible in its definition, is what makes a house more than just a dwelling-place.

Chapter 2

JOHN KYRLE'S COUNTRY

ROSS-ON-WYE is the largest town in the southern part of the county, and nearly all tourists gravitate to it at one time or another when in the area. The older part of the town is built on high ground formed by a red sandstone bluff above the famous Horseshoe Bend of the River Wye, though the original hamlet lay at the far end of the town, right beside the river.

Seen from the north-west Ross makes a beautiful picture, with the slender spire of St Mary's Church stabbing the sky above the clustered roofs and the green of the surrounding trees. Through the flat meadowlands below the river flows slowly, deceptively gentle and peaceful, in wide looping bends as it makes its way down to Goodrich and past Kerne Bridge. From there it makes incredible convolutions round Coppet Hill, Huntsham and Whitchurch until, at Symond's Yat, it enters upon its journey down the famous Wye Valley past Monmouth, Tintern, Chepstow, and out at last into the Severn Estuary. It is because of this that Ross is often called 'the Gateway to the Wye'.

The whole area is full of interest and scenic beauties of its own, quite apart from its famous river, and not least amongst these beauties are the many houses, great and small, which have grown up through the centuries here in this often disputed plot between Wales and England proper. A brief glimpse of some of them may be snatched as the traveller passes by; others are secluded and hidden from the view of the curious eye. But apart from the natural desire for privacy, in the past houses were often tucked away deliberately to escape the unwelcome attention of marauders who frequently roamed the countryside. For here we are near true border country, and the whole area was subject to invasions and incursions from Roman times right up to the bitter days of the Civil War.

There are conflicting theories about the meaning of the name, but the most likely derivation seems to be from the Celtic *rhos* meaning a moor, and not, as is sometimes claimed, a headland or promontory, which would have been *pen.* As already mentioned, the oldest settlement seems to have been down at the lower end of the present town, in what is now known as Brookend, where the inhabitants would have had easy access to the streams flowing into the Wye. The original hamlet would have been mainly of wooden buildings, or wattle and daub, with only a few stone houses even in Saxon times. What in later years was probably a Saxon church near Brookend was destroyed during the wars of King Stephen. The present parish church of St Mary dates in part from *c.* 1200, though mostly from 1287 onwards.

In Norman times Ross became an ecclesiastical manor owned by the Bishops of Hereford, who had their fishing rights in the Wye and their hunting rights 'within the Forest of Penyard'. Both of these privileges were jealously guarded, according to old records, and legal action was taken against any poachers or trespassers. The Bishop's Summer Palace was built on the high sandstone cliffs, affording its residents wonderful views of the Black Mountains in the west, and away to the Malverns in the east.

Ross cannot boast a chamber wherein that much-travelled lady Queen Elizabeth slept, nor where her more boisterous Sire was entertained to the huge feasts he so much enjoyed, but Blount has an interesting note regarding Ross in days long before those worthy monarchs came to the throne. He records: 'In a house which was formerly an Inn, opposite to the King's Head, there is a chamber to this day called "The King's Chamber", where Henry IV slept when he came to see his Queen.' That good lady was at Monmouth where next day she gave birth to their son, the future and illustrious Henry V, and the news reached the King as he was preparing to cross the ferry at Walford on his way out of Ross. Today this house no longer exists, but it is believed to have been nearly opposite the beautiful black-and-white timbered building in the High Street which now houses a chemist's shop and an estate agent's office. This itself is well worth examining, an especially interesting feature being the small carved heads reputed to represent King Charles II.

Linked as Ross is with the famous John Kyrle, the Man of Ross, the great attraction in the town is JOHN KYRLE'S HOUSE, built originally by Walter Kyrle, Barrister-at-Law, *c.* 1620. It stands in the Market Place facing the red sandstone Market Hall, built in 1660-74, and has endured a number of changes since it was John Kyrle's private residence. At one time it was an inn, but now is a chemist's shop. It is a pleasant black-and-white timbered building, and behind it is the garden where John Kyrle used to sit in his quaint stone summer-house, with its strange little gables and lancet windows. He would have been able to look up at the tall spire he had rebuilt for St Mary's; probably he would even have been able to see the trees in the grounds of the Prospect, which he had created where once the Bishop's Palace had dominated the scene. At that time, too, the Rector's House was in the meadow below, and the Vicar's House at the far end of the church, where there was also a clergy house for chantry priests.

In Edde Cross Street stands MERTON HOUSE, still dining out on the fact that Nelson and Lady Hamilton once stayed there. The room reputed to have been their bedroom has a heavily carved and embossed ceiling, and there is a graceful eighteenth-century staircase circling up against the walls of the entrance hall in the style popular in that era. At the far end of the house is a small chapel, now used as a reception area. It was probably added on in the 19th century, and the panelled walls and traceried wooden ceiling still remain. The view from the gardens would have made the Bishop's Palace jealous of competition, had it still been in existence, for Merton House overlooks the lovely sweep of the Wye and the far line of hills to the west and east.

There are several houses of interest to antiquaries in the town, already well listed in the various guide books and leaflets issued by the local tourist office.

At nearby Weston-under-Penyard is WESTON HALL, one of the finest examples of a Jacobean House in the southern part of the county. A glimpse of it can be caught through the tall wrought-iron gates facing on to the A40. It has an air of great charm combined with an uncomplicated dignity, and is built of the warm red sandstone of the locality, with a three-storeyed, gabled porch centrally and bay windows on either side giving it a perfect symmetry. It looks out over smooth green lawns surrounded by a variety of flowering trees and shrubs, and was built by Walter Nourse, originally of Woodeaton in Oxfordshire. In the church nearby is a brass commemorative plaque showing him, a typical, mild-faced Jacobean gentleman, at prayer. He lived to the then extraordinary age of ninety-two years.

Inside, the house is earlier than the exterior indicates, parts of it being Elizabethan. There are traces of an earlier timber-framed building, from which some beams remain, but in general the house as we see it at present is that which was built by Walter Nourse from 1570-80 or so. Originally the old Gloucester Road ran behind the house, between it and the barn and stables, and not along the route of the present A40, which is on the garden side of the house. The face which looks out on to this old road (now part of the drive) has the slightly staid appearance of a typical town house. Only on entering the original driveway would the true front of the house have been seen, its symmetrical and more spacious proportions marking it definitely as a country mansion.

The plan is an *L*-shaped one, with the large porch giving on to the main Hall which still has its original panelling of the late 1600s, moulded ceiling beams and exposed joists. On a table is one of the little models of the house, the making of which were such a popular hobby of late-eighteenth- and nineteenth-century ladies, and for which we owe them a tremendous debt of thanks. So often they retain for us features long since removed, and explain additions which might otherwise be a little preplexing in the context of later years.

On the left, on either side of the large stone open fireplace, are doors leading into the Study and the Dining-room. The dark, wooden, arched doors and door-frames are very unusual, and give a most pleasing and dignified touch to the room. The wide, dark oak staircase with its square carved newels and shaped terminals, is the one which was built into the house in Walter Nourse's day, but it has now been removed from its original position, which abutted into the Dining-room, making for a slightly inconvenient shape. Now, on the right hand side of the Hall, it shows off its beauty to advantage, and at the same time the proportions of the Dining-room have benefited by its removal.

In the Drawing-room, immediately facing the doorway, is a huge stone fire-place – the sort which clearly needed a forest of its own to supply its devouring needs. The panelling in this room is of the William and Mary period and here, as in the Hall and the Dining-room, are the old, exposed ceiling beams, dark with age and great with dignity. The Bedroom over this room has Elizabethan panelling, with a carved and panelled overmantel.

Sheltered by the two wings of the house is the inner courtyard, with two wrought-iron gates piercing the two garden walls, one leading off past the modern addition of 1910-12 built by a local architect, towards the original stable-block. The other leads into the great red-brick walled garden, dating from *c.* 1600. Walter Nourse must have planned and planted his garden with great joy and care once his house was built; and he also planned the entrances to his gardens with considerable care, for the gates have square piers with moulded cappings, and the lovely slender wrought-iron work is topped by the Nourse coat-of-arms and crest. The gate on the far side of the garden, which now opens on to the busy A40, is also an original one, which probably then opened out into fields and orchards beyond. Contrary to general belief the lovely wrought-iron double gateway to the present drive, flanked by impressive square piers with moulded stone cappings, is not eighteenth-century, but was made in the 1920s – an excellent example of the very fine craftsmanship of our own century when called upon to match up with that of earlier periods. The massive cedars on the lawns in front of the house also belie the suggestion they give of centuries of growth since, unbelievably, these wide-spreading giants were planted a mere 150 years ago. I think Walter Nourse would have approved of them. The Nourses seem to have been keen gardeners, and one of Walter's descendants in the late 18th century, Col. John Nourse, gave his name to the Nourse Apple, unfortunately now better known in the United States than in its own homeland.

The Great Barn is mid-sixteenth-century, with an addition of *c.* 1600 at the west end. The walls are mainly rubble, with loop-lights, and the fine roof is of five bays and of the queen-post type. The stables north-west of it are a little later, and on their eastern side is a square-headed doorway with an oval panel dated 1709. The centre of the west side is greatly enlivened by the half-timbered and gabled open-balcony type upper storey which was added in the 1920s, giving a very pleasing appearance and adding considerably to the beauty of what otherwise could have been an ordinary, plain stable-block.

Weston Hall has been in the hands of only three families since it was built: the Nourses, the Partridges, and the Aldrich-Blakes who bought it in 1881. It may well be this that gives it that atmosphere of restfulness and continuity so often found in homes that have not had constant changes of ownership. Certainly here at Weston Hall the impression of a contented security is very strong . . . the sensation of 'a house beloved'.

Nearby is BOLLITREE CASTLE – never a true castle, only a sham; but with a charming story. The main part of the house seems to have been built in the mid-1700s, although parts of the original building date from 1500, or earlier. Bollitree was for centuries owned by the Mayricks, or Merricks, who claimed to have held it in the reign of Richard II. It was left by William Merrick to his nephew Thomas Hopkins of Pencoyd (sometimes called Hopkins Merrick), who died in 1788 and who, in his turn, was succeeded by a nephew, one of the Palmers of Pencoyd.

It is said that the castellated portions were added by Thomas Hopkins. There are two versions of the story. In both, they concern a beautiful girl with whom he had fallen deeply in love. In one, she was a romantic who yearned to live in a castle; so Thomas had a shell built round his inheritance, of simulated battlements and outbuildings crenellated to order. It was to this 'castle' that he brought home his bride, and they lived happily ever after . . . The other version is less cheering. This specifies a Spanish princess who said she could never marry anyone who did not possess a castle. (How Thomas came to be moving in such elevated society is not recorded!) Hastily he erected the dissembling pretences of his fortifications to satisfy the conditions. But when the proud beauty discovered what he had done and what sort of castle was proposed as her home, she immediately rejected him out of hand and the luckless lover retired to his 'Englishman's castle' to live and die a bachelor.

This latter story may well be the truer version, and would explain why Bollitree was left to a nephew and not to a son or daughter. It may also explain the haunting by Thomas's ghost, said to appear on Bollitree lawn – not only, some say, by night, but even by day . . . It would also be interesting to know who is the ghostly lady whose footsteps come up the stairs, along the landing, and into a bedroom. And why does she always come up, but never down? Yet the rooms of the

Queen Anne building are light and spacious and have no sense of mystery or sadness, and the central, older part feels warm and contented with its thick stone walls and low doorways. Tales exist of a secret passage to what was once an old monastic farm lower down the hill (parts of which are incorporated in the Sandiway Hotel), and to the old castle of Eccleswall. The only one explored so far petered out halfway across a field, where its roof appeared to have fallen in, leaving little trace other than a pool of muddy water.

Of warm pink sandstone, with five bays and a hipped roof in which nestle three gabled dormer windows, the north-east aspect of Bollitree Castle is a pleasant example of a Queen Anne house. It is only when the other end of it is seen that one realises how many, and how utterly different, are the styles which combine to make it a most intriguing place. For behind the late-seventeenth-century building lies the older part of the house to which were added, by the luckless lover, the pretences of his castle. There they stand, ogee arches, quatrefoils, battlements and strange little gothic turrets, on house and barn alike – some of them genuine enough, since part of the material came from Penyard Castle and part from a dismantled medieval church in Bristol. For a number of years the story of Thomas Hopkins was discounted, but when the present owners, Mr and Mrs Robin Malim, were having extensive renovations undertaken recently, it was found that in most places the crenellated walls had, in fact, been built up round the original stone walling, some eight to twelve inches outside it, indicating clearly that it was indeed a sham or folly.

Bollitree is, and probably will always remain, a bit of a puzzle, full of questions to which no answers can be traced. But none of them are very sombre problems, and it lies there peacefully in the sunlight, its dovecot gleaming white against the cool darkness of the arcaded building beyond, and its imitation moat stocked with ducks who swim contentedly on its smooth surface.

Not far away, at Upton Bishop, an equally unusual find was discovered a few years ago at UPTON COURT, a typical, squarish house with additions which almost completely disguise its older fourteenth-century origins. But when alterations were in hand, a workman had to go up to the roof for something. What he saw there took his breath away. He went in search of the architect, who was on the site, and took him up to see his find. There, complete, perfect, yet hidden for centuries and obviously forgotten and unrecognised, was a fourteenth-century baronial hall roof. Tie-beams, collar-beams, tops of principals, foiled and pointed-trefoiled windbraces, were all there. It was the sort of find which antiquarians yearn for but seldom come across, something which has remained *in situ* for centuries, unsuspected and unaltered.

On the northern side of Ross is the little hamlet of Wilton, with WILTON CASTLE looking sadly derelict against the brisk smartness of the clustering houses beside it. It is difficult to date the original building, and it is not even certain whether the first one was actually on this site, but it was probably one of the five castles mentioned by Domesday as being in Herefordshire before the Conquest. The other possible siting is where the house known as WILTONDALE stands, down the lane skirting the river. The land here certainly gives the appearance of having been artificially raised at some time to form the large sort of mound on which a fortified building would have stood. It would have been a perfect positioning, standing as it does almost directly beside the old ford, now marked by the remains of the stone Praying Cross. In Duncombe, Wiltondale is said to have been the original seat of the Abrahalls, and was clearly a spot of some significance. But in either place the castle would have been well sited to guard the approaches into Wales, commanding, as both do, not only the roads but the river as well. Of the castle built here at Wilton in Norman times only the shell now remains, the mullioned windows of the southern side indicating a later period of history, probably the 14th century; in 1645 Royalist forces burned it down, even though it was a non-defensible mansion and not a fortified building.

But beside its ruins the hamlet of Wilton continued to thrive in a modest way. There had been a ford from time immemorable, and a ferry as early as 1276. No definite records show when the first bridge was built, but ecclesiastical registers state that a 'great stone public road bridge' was in need of repair here in 1518. Sometime after this date the stone bridge seems to have been swept away by floods, for the next reference is to 'a woode bridge by Rosse'. Did the 'woode bridge' in its turn also get swept away? We only know that for some years a ferry was once more maintained at Wilton by the Lordship of Wilton, until the present bridge was built in 1597-99. Compensation for loss of the ferry was obtained by means of a toll-gate erected on, or at, the entrance to the bridge where *pontage* was taken. Near Wilton Bridge today, in a small *cul-de-sac* formed by part of the old road from Ross to Hereford, stands the OLD TOLL COTTAGE, now a charmingly restored black-and-white timbered building surrounded by a garden riotous with roses. For many years it was unoccupied and due for demolition, its centuries-old timbers covered by stone and brick, its antiquity entirely disguised. From the timbers revealed in the rebuilding process, we may assess that the original Toll House was of the black-and-white style of building associated with Herefordshire, and many of the old original beams and rafters still remain. The owner also preserves a bell found in the grounds, in the hope that it may once have been used to summon the inhabitants to take the toll-money.

Not far from Wilton, as crows fly, though down twisting lanes which make it seem more distant for the motor-car, is Sellack, and CARADOC COURT. An old British camp existed here, and the inference is that the house takes its name from this, linking the place with the great British hero who certainly fought all round these parts. The house itself was purchased by Rowland Scudamore in 1594, and underwent a certain amount of rebuilding, which seems to have continued on into the middle of the following century. Today the bay window, porch and gables at the front of the house are Victorian, but the big bay window at the back is original, and the graceful mullioned windows are for the most part just as they were in their prime. It presents a fascinating appearance, with its blending of different styles of architecture, wooden gables rubbing shoulders with stone ones, black-and white exposed timbering linking up with later stone additions, and windows which seem to be trying to see which can give the better view, stone mullions or wooden-framed ones. Inside is still the great oak-panelled Hall of the earliest period of the house, and though no Knights of the Round Table are ever seen feasting here they would undoubtedly not feel out of place if ever they visited it. Tradition links it with Sir Cradoc Vraich-Vras, or Strong Arm, one of the knights of King Arthur's Table.

A short distance further on, at Hentland, is the farmhouse known as LLANFROTHER, or the Church of the Brothers, commemorating, after all these centuries, the old monastic buildings of St Dubricius's seminary for priests. Under the present farmhouse are cellars, bits of old walling, and indications of ancient buildings which may indeed be connected with that long-ago college of British monks.

But ancient and modern have to live cheek by jowl through all centuries; at the end of the Llanfrother track, where it joins the road right in the very centre of the parish, stands what used to be the old school, now renovated and remodelled into charming HENTLAND HOUSE in which the features of a nineteenth-century school have been cleverly used to recall an earlier age. For the big schoolroom, with its high, arched ceiling and dark beams, has been converted into the Dining-room, and carefully planned and decorated to recall an old baronial hall. All the rooms have been skillfully altered and reconstructed, so that the best use has been made of the once large, impersonal classrooms, and the small Study, now intimate and snug with open fireplace and blazing logs. The old bell-turret has been taken down and now forms an archway, and the old bell, dated 1861, is carefully preserved in the house. The whole is an excellent example of how a difficult building of awkward proportions and shape can, with imagination, be turned into a most pleasing dwelling place, full of character and interest.

All along the banks of the Wye here at Hentland and Hoarwithy the houses are like birds nestling on their perches, being built up above the reach of flood waters, their gardens terraced against the wooded, rocky hillside. Each one is charming, and the whole route is a traveller's joy.

Slightly westward lies GILLOW MANOR, believed to derive its name from the Welsh *cil*, a retreat, and *llwch*, a pool, or, 'the retreat by the pool'. The name is admirably descriptive of this lovely old building. It lies in a deep hollow, sheltered from the south and east by a small hill. Like so many buildings in this part of the country, it faces out towards the far off line of the Black Mountains, watching always for the first signs of marauders sweeping across the Marches into England, whether with the threat of actual war, or, equally serious, of swift pillaging raids when animal stock, stores, and even men, women and children were carried off into the misty Welsh hills, usually never to return. Whether Gillow Manor managed to avoid detection in its secluded situation, or whether it was ever raided, is not known. Possibly silence on the subject in local records augers well, and means that it did remain hidden and secure.

But those who built it left nothing to chance. Thus Gillow Manor is an interesting example of a late-fourteenth-century manor house built in the fortified style popular at the time, encircled by a moat fed from a spring on the hill above, and with a deep, battlemented gatehouse approached by a causeway over the moat. A low, wide arch leads under the gateway to a small inner courtyard. Sometime in the 16th century the gatehouse was partly rebuilt and the north-west wing was added, and in the 17th century considerable rebuilding was undertaken in the north-east and south-east ranges. Later still in the same century the south-east and south-west ranges were again largely rebuilt. Today all that remains of the oldest part of the house is the massive, red-sandstone gatehouse, and the chapel adjoining it. In this latter, now the Music-room, one of the old, two-lighted traceried windows remains, making a very lovely feature in this cleverly adapted and most charming room. In the adjoining room the old, rather small, high, mullioned windows have been replaced by a wide picture window and window-seat, flooding the whole room with light and sunshine and giving a view of the far Welsh hills which would have been the envy of those early watchers. It overlooks the gardens and the wide moat – thirty feet deep in one place – which still skirts this side of the house, mirroring in its placid surface the swaying branches of the willow-tree and graceful shrubs which line its border.

An enigma to antiquarians, the real curiosity of Gillow Manor lies in the strange statue carefully treasured within. With a slight look of bewilderment on its face, worn now and almost featureless with age, its cheeks are still smooth, rounded and gentle, not the sharp features of a man of war, nor a stern ascetic – but those of an ordinary, kindly, everyday man. Who is he, this little man wearing early-fifteenth-century civilian clothing? It has been suggested that it is an effigy of one of the early owners of the manor, but Pevsner and others think it more likely to have been one of the statue-type figures which often filled niches on gatehouses. Less than four feet tall, with legs strangely short, and truncated arms, he remains a mystery. Was he indeed a dwarf, one of the 'wise fools' who served their masters well with wit and wisdom once, or was he one of the children of the house? Was he carved to stand in the chapel as a memorial to one who had known and loved the house? Or was he indeed intended to stand upon the battlemented gateway, above the arch perhaps? If only we knew the original positioning of those tantalisingly truncated arms . . . Like some much humbler Venus de Milo, they exert a fascination because they hide a secret we shall never fathom: one upraised slightly, in blessing perhaps, or to hold a staff or implement indicative of trade or status; the other also held slightly away from the body. Unless memorials of actual people, such figures were probably vestigial racial descendants of ancestral gods, or the old domestic gods, who guarded the home and were supposed to frighten away evil spirits. Certainly the Gillow statue must feel cast in the role of Guardian of the House, and it is good to know he still remains in the house he has successfully watched over for so long.

As might be expected with a house as old as Gillow Manor, it has its ghost but the present owners tell me that it is a long time since it was last heard. Once, night after night, they would hear a woman's footsteps going up the stairs to the attic. There she would seem to be searching for something, moving things about, opening and closing drawers and doors, trotting backwards and forwards in the room above their bedroom. When the steps were first heard the owner went in their direction, and found a blocked up doorway leading into a space which opened out into the attics. The marks still remained where an old staircase, taken out some hundred years previously it eventually transpired, had once fitted into the timbers. Oddly, also, no furniture or trunks were stored in the attics, although the ghostly visitor could be heard rummaging about. But when alterations were undertaken to that part of the house a few years ago the haunting ceased. One wonders why? Was the ghostly lady perhaps seeking that elusive state called Happiness? If so, perhaps she had found it, for happiness flows through the rooms of the old manor like a warm tide of golden sunshine, and the laughter of children echoes through its walls.

Taking the road over the bridge at Hoarwithy towards How Caple, suddenly, across the green pastureland, an old, stone manor house comes into view. This is FAWLEY COURT, built between 1590 and 1621, and probably started by Thomas Gwillim who, at his death in 1604, owned the manors of Fawley and Strangeford. Eventually, by marriage, Fawley came into the possession of the Money-Kyrles of Much Marcle. Later it was sold by them, but it is interesting to note how often the names of Gwillim and Kyrle appear in this part of the country.

Nearly symmetrical in style, it has a canted bay with six-lighted windows, a three-light window, another canted bay identical to the first, another three-light window, and then the square porch thrust forcefully out as though demanding attention as you enter the domains beyond. The windows of the house are unusual for the period, a cross between two styles of building, being transomed, but made lighter and more graceful than usual by the slight arching above them instead of the later, squarer heads. The symmetrical pattern is repeated on the upper floor to some degree, though there are no bays, only four sets of three-lighted windows, and then, over the porch, a two-light one. The effect achieved is one of the most agreeable balance and repose. Inside the house there is a fireback dated 1629 in the Dining-room, and some very good panelling. The door-knocker bears the date 1635.

Almost in front of the house are three interlinked ponds, beautifully land-scaped with borders of shrubs and flowers, with graceful trees admiring their own images in the placid waters below. In spring this lovely spot is idyllic with daffodils and crocuses, and horses roam freely on the pasture lands through which the roadway passes. In autumn, gold and flame of leaves conspire with morning mist to make it seem as though Nature is lighting some secret bonfire of her own. But the greatest surprise of all comes when the slight bend of the road in front of Fawley Court is negotiated, and the back part of the house comes into view. For this is timber-framed, early-sixteenth-century, and probably older than that in some parts. The present owner has added on one of the out-houses at the back to the remainder of the building, making it into living quarters, and thus forming an almost square courtyard. The Tudor aspect here has been kept and the whole character therefore retained most pleasantly.

Perhaps it is the unusual setting in which Fawley Court stands which gives it so much character, with the main road running beside it and through its pasture lands, dividing it from, yet skirting, the lovely ponds to one side of it. It is as though it has somehow spilled its beauty over the country around with a gener-osity which has allowed all comers to partake of its carefully maintained and nurtured glories, natural and man-made.

Cars which go speeding down the winding lane which is in fact the old Ross-Monmouth road, past Duxmere and Hom Green, may pass the lodge-gates to HILL COURT before they realise that they exist. And, if so, they will never see the long, straight drive which leads to the handsome red-brick mansion crowning the eminence of the slight hill, and will have missed one of the really fine houses of Herefordshire, appropriately enough called Hill Court, the home of Mr John Trafford.

Tradition insists that it was John Kyrle, the Man of Ross, who planted the line of elms which ran, until the first attack of elm-disease in 1930-31, parallel with the drive. The story goes that John Kyrle and Joseph Clarke conjoined to plant an avenue of elms from Hill Court all the way to Ross. Now there is a lighter, lacier avenue of white limes, planted not only nearer the drive, but nearer also to our own times, pointing directly to the house, and ending just before the ha-ha and fine vase-topped piers of the entrance gates. Beyond the spacious forecourt lies the fine frontage of the house, built *c.* 1698-1708, and enlarged by the addition of the two projecting wings just before 1750.

The house itself is of warm red-brick, stone quoins emphasising the symmetry of the design, with hipped roofs and balustraded parapets. Over the three central bays is a fine pediment which bears the arms of the Clarke family carved in white stone and flanked by a profusion of fruit and flowers in rich scroll design. The decoration and quality of this pediment go far to soften the slightly severe lines of the central part of the house, and give a graciousness which might not have been achieved by a plain pediment with a geometrical design.

A flight of stone steps leads up to the late-eighteenth-century door, surrounded by well proportioned architraves and pediment over, which links it with the window above. This has balustrading and a canopied heading, not too large, not too small, but just right to draw the attention to the centre of the block and give an air of calm dignity to the whole. One charming touch to welcome the visitor, is the pair of pine-apples, the symbol of hospitality, which top the pier ends of the handrails on either side of the steps.

The west side of the house faces out over lawns and extensive shrubberies, and is similar in design to the front, but without the central scrolled pediment. The garden doorway, somewhat earlier than the entrance door, has plain moulded architraves, but a fine swan-necked pediment over.

It is not known for certain who designed Hill Court, though local legend attributes it of course to the ubiquitous John Kyrle – a sentiment not shared by the present owner. Yet it may well be that Kyrle did at least guide the taste and the final decisions of the two Clarke brothers whose fortunes enabled them to build the original central portion of the house, since one of the daughters, a spinster who died at the age of 92, records the fact that she could remember him often dining at the house during her childhood. Since John Kyrle died in 1724 it is not impossible that he did indulge his taste for building and tree-planting by giving advice to the less sophisticated Clarke brothers, who came initially from a worthy yeoman family, connected by marriage with the Kyrles of the Hill, or Hull, a timbered building across the fields from Hill Court itself and now known as Old Hill Court. From being yeoman farmers, they seem to have 'entered commerce', three sons becoming, respectively, a clothier, a mercer, and a haberdasher. In 1651 Richard Clarke described himself as 'gentleman', and he was granted arms in 1663, so by that time evidently the family had some status. It was his sons, or possibly grandsons, who are believed to be responsible for building Hill Court, or at least the original part now presented by the central block.

Inside, the Entrance Hall has an unusual and attractive flooring composed of grey stone combined with polished green-grey slate. The effect is cool, and gives a touch of that solemnity usually associated with churches and cathedrals of the same period of architecture. But here the walls are lined with beautiful gold-green tapestries bearing the arms of William III. They bring a touch of colour from the 18th century into the oak-panelled room, bright today with bowls of flowers and the grace of period furniture. Behind the Hall rises the fine staircase with its unusual, delicately carved tread-ends and turned balusters, which almost distract attention from the fine plaster ceiling above, rich with the flowers, fruit and scrollwork of the late 17th or early 18th century.

On the right of the Hall is the Morning-room, its wainscot walls painted pale green, and the cream central panels painted with musical and martial trophies. There is an attractive mirrored recess with wood and plaster framing opposite the big marble fireplace, and here again flowers reflect the owner's love of beauty.

This room leads into what was the original withdrawing-room of the house, now known – appropriately anough – as the Cedar Parlour. It is certainly unusual, being panelled in contrasting woods, the red of cedar set against the veneers of walnut, oak, and lighter sycamore and satinwood.

The Dining-room is panelled, with a plain moulded cornice and fine marble mantelpiece; and the Library has a decorated cornice, elegant in its simplicity, and a graceful chandelier, its natural, arching lines reminding one of the Roman fountains. The doors to all the rooms are beautifully proportioned with their height increased by the simple austerity of the architrave headings above, and the whole house has that quality of light and spaciousness which is the glory of English architecture of the period. But the apple-green Drawing-room, with its richly ornamented cornice and ceiling-rose, is a particular delight. Here the chandelier is more impressive and opulent than the gentler grace of the one in the Library, but it suits the richer splendour of the room and its more formal purpose, and in this is greatly aided by the splendid carved mantelpiece. The graceful Venetian window has fluted supporting columns and is crowned by a fine gilded and scrolled plasterwork pelmet above the curtain drapes. The whole imparts an elegance to the room which is entirely in keeping with its period and the Age of Grace in which it was designed.

For connoisseurs of the impermanency of certain styles of art, the Painted Bedroom on the first floor is perhaps the great attraction of Hill Court. This is an example of the late-seventeenth-century Chinoiserie painting which was once so fashionable but passed out of favour fairly quickly. The mouldings of the doors and panels are marbled white, with the Chinoiserie scenes in deep russet brown.

With the death of old Jane Clarke in 1806, the property devolved upon her kinsman, Capt. Kingsmill Evans of the Grenadier Guards, and it would seem to have been from then that the gardens began their rise to their present beauty. Although the interior of Hill Court is not open to the public its grounds are opened twice a year in aid of various charities and are, for all garden lovers, a real delight.

From the broad path bordered by wide herbaceous beds which leads off from the courtyard, the way goes past the big brick, six-sided dovecot, *c.* 1700, and into the old walled garden built at the same date. It was beyond this that Kingsmill Evans designed a new walk from which a view of Goodrich Castle might be seen. The central part of the walled garden is laid out in the form of a parterre, with yews forming slender, trimmed pyramids surrounded by flower beds and with a sundial set in smooth green turf. Wrought-iron gates lead out into the Long Walk beside the yew hedge, which has had 'windows' cut into it at advantageous positioning to gain the best views of the surrounding countryside.

From Kingsmill Evans, Hill Court passed to his nephew, Kingsmill Manley Power and, on his death, was bought by Maj. Lionel Trafford, who was the third son of Mr C. G. Trafford, originally of Staffordshire. When, in the early 19th century, his mansion of Swithamley was burned down after 300 years of family inheritance, Mr Trafford decided to settle in Herefordshire, and acquired Michaelchurch Court, thus beginning the family connection with this county. His third son, Lionel, upon retirement from the Army, bought Hill Court, and on his death in 1900 was succeeded by his younger brother, father of the present owner. And it is largely due to the efforts of the latter that Hill Court and its gardens have been brought up to their present state of beauty. With an unerring eye for aesthetic values, he removed some slightly trivial Victorian trimmings – stained glass windows unsuitably placed and of doubtful quality, and a conservatory which unbalanced the symmetry of the west side of the house. However, it is mainly in the gardens that his work may be appreciated by the public, and perhaps especially in the water gardens which lead, by quiet pools and lingering streams, past a magnificent collection of aquatic plants, down to the little Chinese pavilion which mirrors its grey colours and slender columns in the water below. Its slight form at the far end of the water garden might almost be intended as a deliberate, even gently ironic, contrast to the sturdy stone dovecot towering watchfully over the head of the water garden. On the north side of the house a broad grass avenue leads to the white Gothic summer-house set against the deep green of the trees beyond, and there are beautiful glades of rare and valuable trees and shrubs, as well as a small formal garden round a lily pond with steps leading up to one of the many classical statues which adorn the lawns.

Herefordshire is not rich in 'great' houses, as the term is usually understood. There are no Blenheims or Burghleys, no Hardwicks or Hopetowns. But she is rich in one particular field, namely, that her architectural heritage consists of houses, such as Hill Court, which were built to live in and not simply to impress. They are evidence for a way of life actually lived, not enacted; and homes which were used, not merely visited perhaps once a year or less. There is about them all, in this respect, a feeling of warm reality which is often lacking in some of the vast, palace-like structures of England.

Goodrich Castle may be framed by the peepholes in the lovely yew hedge at Hill Court, but a smaller house, almost under the shadow of the castle, cannot be seen from them. Yet in its own way it too is full of interest. Y CRWYS, or The Cross, to give it the Anglicised version of its charming Welsh name, is a small, somewhat mysterious building lying near Ye Hostelrie Hotel at Goodrich, and connected by history with the Castle itself, many believe. It is a strange little building, with an apse-like projection at the back and an outer staircase leading up to a door in the wall. These features, together with a jutting out chimney-piece all support the tradition that originally it was a chapel and place of rest for priests and pilgrims making the journey down to Tintern, using the old road over the ford, past the Castle and the little house, and then on towards the great Abbey. Over the doorway, in a tiny gable, is a stone crest, showing eleven birds, believed to be herons.

It is this crest which makes the second version of its origins seem a little less likely than it might appear on the surface, for this insists that it was a gaolhouse. (Not many families would wish their personal crest to appear on a gaol.) Probably the truth lies somewhere between the two: the style of building certainly seems to imply that the chapel story has foundation, and then later, sometime after the Dissolution, the small building may have been used as a gaol – some older inhabitants say even up to within living memory. Their grandparents had spoken of stone slabs round the walls which had been the sleeping places for the old monkish travellers. But whatever the truth behind the theories, inside the house is now a pleasant, happy home, three storeys high, with a kitchen basement, a living room on the ground floor, and bedroom upstairs, in the small priest's room above the chapel. In the garden pieces of the old Roman road sometimes come up to the light of day, reminding us of the circling ages which pass, and rise again, in almost reincarnatory rhythm outlasting all the life spans of mere men.

When we turn eastwards, away from the call of the high hills to the west, we find that there is a tremendous difference in the countryside, a difference in buildings, historic remains, even in the people and the atmosphere. In these eastern parts of Herefordshire there are far more pre-history earthworks than in the west, where there are more of the fortified manor-cum-castle stone buildings still remaining. In the east, again, medieval earthworks are comparatively rare, though there are a number of homestead moats, a few mottes, and moated castles at Bronsil and Ashperton, with, of course, the modern EASTNOR CASTLE.

I suppose it might be true to say of Eastnor Castle that it has to be seen to be believed – certainly to be appreciated.

It stands on the slope of the hill, looking out over thickly wooded grounds and away to the high range of the Malvern Hills. Local tradition asserts that it was here that, after the storming of British Camp by the Romans, Caractacus made his last great stand before moving to the line of the far-off village encampments to the west, and engaging in what we today would regard as guerilla warfare. Eastnor is a massive stone structure which might easily have been planned and built by one of the Plantagenets themselves. Instead, it was in fact built in 1812, in the time of the great revival of interest in Gothic architecture which swept England and the Continent. There is an interesting note in Lord Somers's diary of 23 June 1812:

> 'I laid this day the first ashlar ornamental stone, many neighbouring gentlemen and their families being present, and placed under it a piece of Queen Elizabeth (I believe half a crown), my family having settled in Eastnor in that reign; and also a three shilling bank token of the year 1811, when the foundations of Eastnor Castle were marked out and begun.'

From the south east the castle is seen across the mirroring waters of the great lake, a magnificent building with a central keep and massive round turrets at the four corners. The first Lord Somers wanted it to be in the style of a great medieval baronial hall, and the final results must have been very gratifying, since the general effect was certainly achieved.

Eastnor had replaced the earlier family residence of Castleditch, or Ditch House, which in its turn had been the successor to Bronsil Castle, the ruins of which may still be seen in the grounds.

The great structure is of grey stone, embattled throughout, and on the north-west side the arched main gateway is flanked by two round guard-towers, forbidding enough in their severe design to ward off any attack long before it even began, I suspect. All the oak needed for the floors, doors, and panelling was provided from the estate itself, whilst stone from a local quarry was used for several of the main chimney-pieces, being polished to achieve a marble-like finish. Another unusual feature of Eastnor deserves notice. Owing to the shortage of wood, which was needed for building the ships to counter the threat of a Napoleonic invasion, the architect, the famous Sir Robert Smirke, R.A., decided to use cast iron stanchions to replace the usual wooden roof trusses. These are still in perfect condition, and it is said that Eastnor was the first house to have metal roof trusses instead of the traditional wooden ones.

Clearly Sir Robert Smirke intended that his designs for Eastnor should be on the grand scale of Lord Somers's expectations, and he seems to have been lavish indeed in his plans, with regard both to the actual building and to interior decoration. The shock of the death of Lord Somers's heir in action in the Pensinsular War meant that some of the latter was never actually begun and the work at Eastnor slowed down for some time. Later the second Earl pressed forward with the plans again, and the third Earl added greatly not only to the treasures in the house itself, but also to the beautifying of the grounds, which were enriched by the addition of many rare and valuable plants, shrubs and trees.

The Great Hall is a surprise in many ways. The round arches of the doorways stand out white against the dark gleam of the wooden doors and decorated upper walls. Above them, perhaps more in the style of the ecclesiastical clerestories of a cathedral than as usually envisaged in baronial halls, the slender, polished pillars of the arches of the gallery running round the sides of the Hall give an effect of lightness and elegance not usually associated with the earliest periods of great halls. Designed by George Gilbert Scott, today this vast room houses a collection of armour, the various specimens of which have come from all European countries as well as from India, Persia and Africa. It includes complete standing suits of armour, dating from 1530, and also a number of three-quarter suits, for the most part Italian and *c.* 1580 onwards. An old bullion chest, said to have come from one of the ships of the Spanish Armada, a whole variety of swords and other weapons, together with many other items of general historic interest, are also here; but the most elaborate suits of armour are in the Inner Hall. Of particular interest to this part of the country is the suit worn by the King's Champion (of the famous Dymock family of nearby Dymock) at George IV's coronation banquet.

The Dining-room has a slightly arched and painted ceiling, its wooden beaming dividing it into large panels, each containing shields of the arms and quarterings of the various families connected with Lord Somers's family, the Cocks. Around them are sprays of oleanders and bay, symbolising the laurel which is the Somers badge. Above the half-panelling of the walls is a collection of portraits of famous characters of the 17th century, mostly by Van Dyck, Lely and Romney, together with a number of family portraits.

The Gothic Drawing-room could really be called by no other name, with its rich, almost flamboyant fan-tracery rearing itself ecstatically up to the painted and gilded ceiling. The gilded coats-of-arms displayed show the connection of the Somers family with the Plantagenets, Berkeleys, Russells, Treadways, and Nashes. Above the big stone open fireplace is a family tree, and the great brass chandelier in the centre of the room was designed by Pugin after the original in Nuremberg Cathedral.

Other family portraits in the Octagon Saloon are by Romney, Watts, Reynolds, with one by Angelica Kaufmann, that great fore-runner of feminine equality.

In the Long Library the ceiling is again painted, this time with the Virtues and their opposite Vices. The tapestries here came from a palace in Mantua and represent Roman Triumphs. Below them are shelved the great collection of over 5000 volumes which came from the library of Dr Treadway Nash. Fine chandeliers hang down the centre of the room, which is 63 feet long and has two stone fireplaces in it. Perhaps they are an invitation to study the volumes so carefully amassed here, but the Little Library is a more intimate room, and probably used more often for that purpose. Over the chimney-piece there is a large pearwood mirror, enchantingly carved by that master of the art, Grinling Gibbons.

The grounds of Eastnor can no longer be maintained in the grand style of former years, but they are nonetheless very beautiful. Caractacus and the Druids may not haunt the grounds of Eastnor, where once so long ago they lived and roamed, but no doubt if they were to do so they would be well pleased with all they found.

Perhaps the town which visitors remember as being most typical of the black-and-white timbering associated with Herefordshire is Ledbury, on the eastern borders. There are too many buildings here to list, and plenty of good handbooks about the town, so only titbits can be given to whet the appetite. But the building everyone seems to remember, partly because of its prominent position right on the main street, is LEDBURY PARK, the former Herefordshire home of the Biddulphs. The west front, the oldest part of the building, dates from the 16th century and is a mass of neat, narrow timbering, each floor projecting a little over the one below. Its windows are made impressive with deep moulded surrounds and pilastered sides to the architravure. The upper storey was added in the first part of the 17th century, and has five gables on the western face and one on each of the south and north ends. The timbering is in keeping with the lower storeys, but the northern range, built at the same time, displays the wider, square timbering then popular. The stables, and the lodge, east of the house, are an addition of the early 18th century. Inside the house there are moulded ceiling beams, some original panelling, and the date 1590 over a doorway.

A little further down the main street THE FEATHERS HOTEL bristles with narrow timber-framing along its entire front. Originally two houses, now joined together, the south block is an interesting example of a four-storeyed building, rare in these parts. It was built *c.* 1560–70 and the top storey, which overhangs slightly as do the other two, was added in the early 17th century, when the second of the two houses was built, or rebuilt. This, with its three storeys, would then have been a few feet taller than the first. In what looks suspiciously like a case of competition another floor was added, five gabled, and overtopping the new house by a few feet. 'Anything you can do, I can do better' was a game played even in the 17th century, apparently. It seems likely that the same architect was used here as at Ledbury Park, for the added upper storey has the same style of gables though the actual design of the timber-work is different.

THE CHURCH HOUSE, in Church Lane, is entirely charming, with its four gables above a central, lower, projecting gable with a semi-octagonal bowed and diamond-latticed window. The original entrance is below the overhanging bow window, and has carved supports to the little projecting bay above. It is a delightful house in a delightful lane, and this little projecting bay gives it an air of added importance, as though it were there to keep watch and guard over the rest of the houses and ensure their utmost propriety.

A house which should also be mentioned, and may be seen coming in from Gloucester on the right, is DINGWOOD PARK, built late in the 17th century on a square plan with a small projecting wing on the south-east side. The exterior is perhaps unexceptional, being typical of its age and pleasantly symmetrical, with a hipped roof and, unusually, a central window over the main door which is narrower than the two on either side of it. It is perhaps the plaster ceiling work inside which is of special interest. From the formation of the Drawing-room ceiling it would seem probable that the house was originally built in the style then popular in the county, where the entrance was direct into the hall or dining-room, with the parlour, or withdrawing-room, leading off from one side. The simpler, more austere lines of the eight panelled ceiling (of which two panels now form the Entrance Hallway), compared with the richer ornamentation of the ceiling in the left-hand room, seem also to indicate this. What would have been the original parlour has a very lovely plaster ceiling divided into three main panels, of which the midmost one has a central wreath of fruit and flowers, with floral sprays in the quadrant angles. In the side panels, again sub-divided into threes, are branches of oak and bay. There is a moulded panelling along the walls, with a dado-rail and stone fireplace. The oak and bay motif is repeated in the Study, and the south-west Bedroom has a plaster ceiling similar to that in the room below. Once again, it is the house of a comfortable, unostentatious country gentleman who loved beauty, but not vulgar display of wealth, and in whose life pleasant living was nicely balanced with a dignified simplicity.

1. **Weston Hall**. The front face, a pleasing example of Jacobean architecture

2. **Bollitree Castle**. The Queen Anne house, with sham battlements behind and castellated outbuildings

3. Gillow Manor. The late-fourteenth-century battlemented gateway mirrored in the waters of the moat

4. The Old Toll Cottage at Wilton

5. Hill Court. The water-garden and Chinese pavilion

6. Fawley Court, built 1590-1621, showing the unusual arching of the transomed windows

7. **Hill Court**, built *c.* 1698–1708 for the Clarke family. The two wings of this imposing frontage were added *c.* 1750

8. **Hill Court**, the Drawing-room. The plasterwork of the moulded cornice, ceiling rose and scroll-worked pelmets is a particular feature

Chapter 3

THE REGION OF ARCHENFIELD

THE area from Ross-on-Wye down through Llangarron to the Monmouth border at Ganarew, is rich in names which indicate its Welsh ancestry. Within a comparatively small area there are some fifteen houses or areas with the prefix *tre-*, meaning 'the homestead of' or, eventually, house or home. It is sometimes said that this is used only for the dwelling of the chieftain of a tribe. There are indications, however, that it was not always the 'chief chief' but sometimes something more akin to the 'chief assistant to the assistant chief' – in other words, the head of one of the branches of the clan who yet owed allegiance to one ultimate chieftain. An interesting corroboration of this theory is to be found here in the Llangarron area. All around we find the *tre-* prefix. Treworgan, Trebandy, Tre-erven, Trewen, Tretire, Trevase, Treberon, and others. And, almost in the centre of them all, is a farm with the odd-sounding name of Trippenkennett. Though it may sound as though it has closer connections with Rumplestiltskin and Scandinavian fairy tales than with Welsh history, it is, in fact, a corruption of *Tre-pen-cenedl*, meaning 'the homestead of the chief of the clan', and was, originally, clearly the home of the tribal group's headman.

Here also are many *llan-* names, indicating a very old foundation, nearly always connected with a sacred spot, an enclosure in which a holy man often lived (long before even the British Church had taken root in this land), and then ultimately, a church. The church and area of nearby Ganarew, for instance, take us back to a link in the early sixth-century; for Ganarew is said by some to be a corruption of St Gwynog, who was the son of Gildas, the early writer usually best remembered for his *Liber Querulus*, or 'Complaining Book' – an unfortunate fame to follow a man through so many centuries. Another derivation is *Geneu y Rhiw*, 'the mouth of the valley on the slope of the hill' or, according to another version, 'the jawbone of the hill'. It is difficult to know which is the most likely, or whether they are in fact all partly true and combined.

The old Roman road down to Caerleon came through the narrow pass here at Ganarew, and undoubtedly a road was here long, long before the Romans came. Up on the top of the Doward there was a Roman signal station on the spot where, earlier, an old Iron Age British encampment had been.

Geoffrey of Monmouth mentioned Ganarew as the place where Vortigern had his castle 'in the county of Archenfield, upon the river Gwy, on the mountain that is called Doward', and where he was besieged by Ambrosius (possibly Arthur) until he finally perished in the burning citadel. King Arthur's Cave, on the side of the Doward, probably perpetuates that action in folk-memory.

Those days are lost in the Dark Age of our History but it is certain that there was a settlement here at Ganarew in very early times, since it is recorded in *Domesday*.

Standing beside the tiny church is THE OLD MANOR HOUSE, a long white building which has grown through the centuries. The oldest part now remaining dates back to the 16th century, but the house which stood here before that can be traced back to 1266. At one time it was a priory, though it is not known under what religious order. The marks of the old encircling wall can still be seen, but there is no other visible evidence of the old community buildings. At the back, where the sixteenth-century building ends, may be seen the portion added on in the days of Good Queen Anne, followed by the Victorian addition, and then the modern part *c.* 1930, which juts out and makes a slight sheltering bay to the east side of the courtyard.

Inside are old beams which have seen 300 years or more go by, and a secret room was found built into the roof, perhaps to shelter one of the Catholic priests who frequented the area. But perhaps the strangest thing about the Old Manor House is its ghost – one of those friendly, family types who belong in some sense to a house even more than its living inhabitants. Several people have sensed a presence, some have heard it, and one person who saw it described it as a man wearing a tall black hat, black cloak and high black boots, somewhat in the manner of the Stuart era. He appears to come down the stairs from the attics, down the next flight, and across to the front door which he opens and closes behind him, his footsteps echoing as he walks across to the far side of the courtyard. Who is he? No one knows and no clue has ever been found to give any hint as to his identity.

Visible from the dual-carriageway a short distance along the road to Ross is SELLARSBROOKE PARK, which has been described as one of the finest specimens of a family-type Georgian house in the county. Its links with history go back at least to Roman times, for when building work was undertaken a few years ago the remains of a complete Roman hypocaust were found; so perfect were they that they could even today have formed the central heating system of that part of the house. Quite evidently a Roman building of some size stood here, right beside the old, deeply-cut track which must have been old when Rome discovered it, and this building was probably either a sizeable villa-farm or a military establishment. The latter seems more likely, since on old maps Sellarsbrooke is called 'The Fort'. The cellar walls are seven feet thick in places, unusual in ordinary domestic cellars, and this confirms the belief that a dwelling of some sort has stood here for nearly 2000 years. The back part of the house shows indications of Tudor construction; and exterior stone cladding was found recently on what are now interior walls, more evidence that the Georgian portion was added to an older building which, in its turn, had probably been built on to, or over, an even earlier dwelling.

It seems that somewhere between 1740 and 1790 a captain of the Royal Navy decided to build himself a house with his prize-money, and to build it on here to front the old Tudor house. Whether this belonged to his family, or whether he came new to the district and, with an eye for beauty, decided he could not improve on the situation, is not known. But he built his new house here, looking out southwards to the Doward, with panoramic views stretching away eastward and soft rolling hills to north and west. At some slightly later date its fine, four colonnaded Palladian-style portico and plain pediment was added, bringing immense importance to the otherwise plain façade. Around1825 the Marriott family came to live here, and Charles Marriott changed the name to Sellersbrook. Through a variety of changes it has now at last stabilised itself as Sellarsbrooke Park. The original estate must have been considerable, since at one time Goodrich Castle was part of the dowry of a daughter of the house, and even today it owns Commons Rights at Crickhowell and Tretower. It is believed that at one time it was owned by Sir William Wyntour.

Today the shining white frontage with its five bays and stately Ionic-column portico stands high on its hill, looking out serenely over the lake far down below. The double doors, set in an arched surround, are framed by glazed and traceried side- and fan-lights in the Adam style; the Entrance Hall is wide and welcoming, with its gleaming white and black flooring, and the white of its pilasters and arched ceiling thrown into contrast against the vivid orange of its walls. The interior exhibits many unusual features for a family house of this size and period, and though the architect and builder are unknown it is evident that neither taste nor financial resources were lacking.

The Drawing-room, entered through rosewood double doors, has a charming moulded ceiling, its white, circular, almost cob-webby design cleverly thrown into relief by the three varying shades of yellow of the ceiling itself. This contrast is continued throughout the room, which is on two levels, with two shallow steps set between four fluted Adam columns leading up to the Music-room. The slightly curved inner wall here, occasioned by the central, oval stairwell of the house, adds to the interest of shape and proportion. Beyond lies the Library, light and pleasant with its white shelves and turquoise blue walls adding to the warm, rich colours of the books themselves. A secret or concealed doorway here provides a short cut through into the central Hall of the house.

Beyond the Library lies the Study, and here we are in the oldest part of the house, the remains of the original Tudor building, much altered to admit sunlight and to allow access to the courtyard and garden beyond. One old, arched wooden door remains, together with the huge, bricked-up archway which once housed a massive similar door leading onto the lane outside. Here again, as everywhere through the house, the present owners' love of light and colour is evident, and one feels that work done in such cool, bright surroundings can never feel like drudgery or penance.

Like the Drawing-room, the Dining-room has a magnificent chandelier suspended from a similar, fluted design on the ceiling. Here the mouldings are picked out in white against three shades of blue, and a glance at the far end of the room explains why it could indeed have been no other colour, for here is a fine, and very unusual, Wedgwood fire-surround with side columns and centrepiece in blue, and the traditional classical figures gracing the whole. The deep green damask wallpaper presents a perfect foil for the airy grace of the Wedgwood part of the scheme. Here, too, is a concealed door leading into the little room which the family regard as their private sanctum, and which was probably the original morning-room of the house. Here the décor is bold purple contrasting with the shining white of the fluted wall pilasters which add so much to the interest of the room; and French windows lead out into the garden.

Both the central, oval Inner Hall and the Staircase itself are unusual and charming in their concept. For the Hall lies under a fine lantern in the roof, two floors up, which is enriched with a petalled, circular moulding in white and orange; and whilst most Georgian flying staircases spiral gracefully round the walls, this one is oval and leads to the first floor landing. Here the oval shaping is pointedly emphasised by the four white, panelled doors, which are themselves curved to fit in with the unbroken sweep of the line. Through these curved doors the North and South Galleries are entered, from which lead off the bedrooms of the house, before the staircase continues its upward flight towards the top storey and the little balcony below the lantern.

At the back, double doors lead out into a small, circular courtyard enclosed on half its circumference by the walls of the house itself, and with two curved flights of steps leading up, behind the Italian style fountain, into the flat, rectangular courtyard beyond. It makes the perfect final touch for this spot which once knew a Roman life-style within its confines. One may imagine that the atrium was here, or the colonnaded garden, where Roman ladies grew the roses that reminded them of home.

Above, in the paved courtyard, is the Stable wing, westward facing, not yet renovated. The bare, unfinished walls, when I saw it, reminded me more strongly of the early style of the Roman tradition than do the finished, graceful lines of neo-classical seventeenth- and eighteenth-century buildings. I hope it will be left with its slightly severe, unadorned, early-Roman aspect, looking out over the paved courtyard towards 'the neck of the valley', to remind those who see it of the old Roman building which once stood on this site guarding the approaches leading to Caerleon.

That this area knew considerable Roman activity and culture is emphasised by the fact that several Roman finds have been unearthed. The most notable perhaps is the Llangarron Hoard, found in 1912 in the grounds of the Hill Farm, Llancloudy. It comprised over 3000 coins, and in 1926 they were sent to the British Museum for examination. 650 of them were retained by the Museum and the other 2,500 are now in Hereford Museum. They were found in a couple of urns in a marshy dip beside one of the roads on the farm which seems to have led direct to Pembridge Castle, a mile away, and may well have been a Roman road – certainly the Romans used it. It is interesting to notice on maps that it appears to have linked up with the old road beside Sellarsbrooke just at the entrance to the Ganarew valley where a fort would indeed have been strategically placed.

Only a short way down the old, probably even pre-Roman trackway lies LEWSTONE HOUSE. There was, and to some extent remains, a whole complex of buildings clustered round the original house, including a brew house, now gone, a granary, a laundry cottage, now converted into a charming house, and the various barns, stables and outbuildings needed in the busy life of a well-run farm. The memory of the old, self-supporting units of the Roman villa way of life has never been quite lost in places such as this, which is fairly isolated and which would at one time, even up to the first quarter of this century, have been almost a hamlet on its own – a living community forged by all who lived, worked and formed their own way of life here, their own pleasures and entertainments, too.

The name Lewson, Lewstone, or Lewston, comes from the *Hlæw* of the Old English, meaning a hill; its oldest form seems to indicate 'a hamlet on the hill', or 'stony hill'.

The earliest part of the present house was built *c.* 1500, but almost certainly it is somewhat earlier. In *Cooke's Visitation of Hereford, 1569*, Lewson is mentioned as being owned by David Gwillim, son of Hopkin, and this reference is believed to date back to the 14th century. According to a deed of 1569, Reginald William Vaughan sold his 'principal messuage where he commonly dwelt, lying in Lewson and Ganarew', to Sir William Wyntour (probably an ancestor of the Cavalier whose name is preserved in Wyntour's Leap, near Chepstow) and so Lewson was evidently 'on the map' even then. In 1584 the house was sold to Phillip Jones of Trellyche Grange, Monmouthshire, and at the beginning of the 17th century it came into the possession of a family named Fisher, who undertook extensive alterations and additions, particularly on the south-west side of the central block. They must also bear responsibility, I fear, for the loss of the old mullioned windows and their replacement by the more fashionable but far less interesting wooden frames. A room in the old part of the house, known as 'The Boys' Kitchen' and the Dining-room today, has a fireback with the date 1637 on it, the initials T.F., believed to represent Thomas Fisher, and decorations of fleurs-de-lis.

The oldest part of the house lies beside the road and was built on a modified *H*-plan, with a pleasant belled roof of good proportions. During the Fisher family's occupation the large barn was built, a seventeenth-century building composed of five bays and having trussed rafters and collarbeams in the roof. Beyond the garden wall in front of the house lies the old carriage and stable block, with the groom's living quarters above, and a pony stable and its tiny tack-house at one end near the garden gate.

Early in the eighteenth-century Lewstone appears to have passed into the hands of the Brown family, who intermarried with the Philpotts, of The Sonke, now Llangarron Court. It was purchased by Philip Hoddell in 1919, when the Brown family died out leaving no direct heirs. Earlier, as a tenant farmer there, Sergeant Philip Hoddell had one evening waved goodbye to his family as he rode off to the Boer War, leaving the cluster of buildings he loved so well to join up with other men of the neighbourhood on Crocker's Ash nearby. It is good to know that he returned safely from South Africa and lived on in the area, continuing to farm at Lewstone until he was 80, and dying at the age of 90 in 1963. He was known as an excellent shot and won many cups in the area. The family still have the silver tobacco box presented to him with the spring-lid bearing the legend: 'County of Gloucester Imperial Yeomanry. S.Africa 1899-1901. Sergt. P. Hoddell'.

A matter of interest arises out of an article in the *Monmouth Beacon* of 5th June, 1959, which deals with the visit of the Monmouth Field Club and Antiquarian Society to Lewstone. One sentence reads as follows: 'It might reasonably have been expected that, like Llanrothal and The Cwm, Catholic priests would have found sanctuary here in the 17th century, but records are silent on this point.' Since then, however, a secret room has been found in the loft during building alterations; and there is also a hollow beam in the rafters with a flap which lifts off, leaving room for muskets and ammunition or other articles to be securely secreted within.

Linked, as so many houses are in this area, by marriage, is WHITCHURCH OLD COURT, which was the old manor-house of the Gwillims. In the time of Queen Elizabeth Old Court came into possession of the Gwillims by the marriage of Thomas Gwillim, of Trepencenant in St Weonards, to the co-heiress, Barbara Powell of Whitchurch, who brought Old Court for her dowry. This was not the first time the two families had been united in marriage, for an old document records that sometime at the beginning of the 16th century 'John Gwillim of

Fawley, son of David Gwillim of Lewson in Llangarren, married Joan, daughter of Robert Powell of Whitchurch and had a daughter and heir who married Humphrey Baskerville, youngest brother of Sir James Baskerville of Eardisley'. And Bradney's *History of Monmouthshire* records that 'Old Court in Whitchurch belonged to the Powell family and was inherited by Rudhall Gwillim, whose son Richard Gwillim was born in 1629', Rudhall being the son of Thomas and Barbara Gwillim mentioned above.

From then on it continued in the family until the time of General Wolfe, when Colonel Thomas Gwillim was badly injured in Canada and died whilst on the journey home. A baby daughter was born shortly after, and given the unusual name of Elizabeth Posthuma. As sole heiress she owned Old Court until her marriage to Lt-Gen. John Simcoe, and it passed eventually to their son.

To day it is a hotel, owned by Mr Don Saunders, and even though no longer a family home its original dignity may still be discerned. Tucked away in the recesses of its well-padded form are two priest's holes; and a third is known to exist as well as, it is believed, a secret underground passage.

The main part of the house is probably sixteenth-century, though some roof trusses indicate that parts of an earlier building were incorporated in the later house. Further additions were made during the 16th century and in the 17th century, when the fine stone porch was added. It is a dignified old house, a typical example of a stone built manor, now in the form of an irregular letter *E*, with the old baronial hall still forming the central core.

The oak door in the porch leads directly into a central Entrance Hall, now paved with flagged stones, but once having oak floorboards. The door on the left leads into the original Great Hall, double-storeyed, with old beams and shaped wall posts still in position. An old mullioned window still looks out over the courtyard at the front of the house and opposite is a massive open stone fireplace. Massive it is, and massive many a man must have hoped its walls would prove, as he clambered up into the small priest-hole secreted within the chimney-breast. The Lounge Bars have still the great beamed ceilings of the original rooms, giving character and intimacy to the setting, and log fires still blaze in the old stone fireplaces as they must have done for so many centuries.

Yet when Mr Saunders took over the house it was almost derelict. Of those less happy days no hint now remains. Upstairs the Long Gallery has been re-opened, making a doorway once again where formerly a wall had been added, and within the many bedrooms in this part the old world character of a manor house still exists. Built out at the back is a large new wing housing the huge Elizabethan Room, designed in the style of a Tudor banqueting hall where now, two or three times a week, old tallow candles and huge log fires set the scene for the Elizabethan-style feasts which have become popular. Costumed serving wenches and minstrels bring the atmosphere of another age into the huge room, and many of the items in the feast are real old English recipes, often dating back to Tudor times.

An odd story relates to the discovery, by chance, of the second priest-hole. The workmen had joked about a ghost they called 'George'. He had never been seen but nonetheless all felt there must be a ghost somewhere about. Then one day, breaking through a wall to link up with a passage on the other side, they found themselves staring instead into a small hole from which some sort of chute shot away downwards into the darkness. It was all very fascinating, and they discussed it, probing the walls, and deciding what an excellent means of escape it was for a man trapped on the first floor of a house and yet able to catapult himself down to at least ground level and out to freedom. In the general excitement Mr Saunders's father lost his grip on his hammer, and it slid down the chute into the darkness below. It was a special hammer and he was not amused at loosing it. In the end it was decided to throw a rope down so that a man could slide down, retrieve the hammer and then be hauled up. The rope was thrown down and then hauled up again to check the length . . . Attached to the loop at the end of it, slotted into position and carefully pulled taut, was the hammer. A lucky shot in a million? An unseen agent trying to be helpful? The mystery was never solved, and each man kept his own opinions on the subject, but fewer jokes are made about 'George' now.

A more objective find, perhaps, was a block of wood hidden under the floorboards, carved with the names of workmen, together with a photograph of the group. It was eventually possible to trace them all, and Mr Saunders invited them to the Great Banquet arranged for the house-warming, so that all were together there, those who had worked on the house fifty years or more ago, and those who worked and lived in it today – just as, centuries ago, all gathered to eat in the Great Hall day by day in a form of democracy which had not yet sought to strangle itself by the formation of guilds and unions.

Some houses seem to have an extraordinary effect on those who live in them, twining themselves round hearts and memories much as ivy clings around a tree, and giving a warmth of affection which never dies. Such a one is GREAT TREWEN, standing a little west of Llangarron, and now in the parish of Llangrove, but not visible from the road. Once there may have been a small hamlet up here known simply as 'Trewen', since today there is a Great Trewen, Symond's Trewen, Little Trewen, and Trewen Cottage, all within a short distance of each other. *Gwyn*, from which *wen* comes, means white, or whitened. It is sometimes used for old stone houses, and the probability is that they were whitewashed and so stood out dramatically against the fields and trees and the more usual timber type houses. Matthew's *Continuation of Duncombe's History* states that the name means 'White Town', though a few pages earlier he has described *tre* as meaning 'the homestead of', which is the usually accepted origin. The 'town' aspect in this case is interesting, since there seem to have been traditions that once Trewen was more than just the name of a house, but rather a small settlement. A deed of 1640 mentions a John Phillips, yeoman, of Trewen. And a little further down the lane is a cross roads known as Cross Trehir, or 'the cross-roads by the long-house'. A former owner, Mr Fodin, believes this referred to the old house of Great Trewen, since there was never anything else here which could have been called a long-house in the Welsh sense of the word.

The oldest part of Great Trewen, that nearest the driveway, is pre-Elizabethan; the central part is Elizabethan; and the far end was added in the 17th century. Once there were mullioned windows, but these were in so bad a state of repair that they have had to be replaced, sadly, by modern ones. Once also, an old inhabitant said, there were two pillars and a porch which have long since disappeared. In the oldest part there are still old beams and crucks said to have come from oaks in the Forest of Dean. In the later portions, some of the beams are reputed to be old ships' timbers. During alterations some time ago the original underlying wattle and daub walling was revealed and found to be of split willow instead of the more usual round hazel wattle.

A right-of-way went straight through the house in Elizabethan times, and because of this the front door is directly in line with the back door as the right-of-way had to be maintained. Great Trewen was always a farm; under the granary to the left of the house was a cider mill and press, still in working order, though unused. A small building behind the house used to be the brewhouse; and drains from the busy dairy ran through what is now the living-room.

At LITTLE TREWEN there is a fine fourteenth-century archway in a house which looks as though it was once a far larger, more imposing building than it appears today, possibly a monastic-type house. But, lovingly restored and renovated, it must be much easier to run today than ever it would have been in what seems to have been the old, *L*-shaped plan of the original, larger building.

Further on along the old trackway which still continues its way from Ganarew and Lewson, just above the junction of the lane at Ruxton Green, lies RUXTON HOUSE, originally Ruxton Chapel. It is an almost perfect site, on the little hill above the Garron Brook, where once the congregation were baptized in the stream. Built of stone, with a Westmoreland slate roof, it has a columnaded portico which escapes being pretentious because the simple but dignified proportions make it entirely appropriate to its surroundings. The marks of the old arched chapel doorway are still visible under the canopy and above the present door. The remains of an arched window above the Holy Table can still be seen in the east wall of the house. At the west end was a cottage for the caretaker and his family. Now made into one large, open area downstairs, it makes a very lovely room with its old elm beams uncovered and its stonework, long hidden under plaster, now repointed and displaying a range of beautifully muted shades.

The history of the house is interesting. About the year 1800 the Revd Thomas Jones, an Anglican clergyman residing at Whitefield nearby, attended a gathering at a farm in Whitchurch called The Malt Shovel (it had once been a public house) in order to hear a well-known preacher from the Independent Church at Ross, the Revd William George. He was so affected by the sermon then heard that, an old record says, 'he wept like a child . . . and became quite another man.' Having considerable estates in the area, and becoming convinced that the parochial system of the Church of England frequently left much of the Gospel unpreached, he determined to build a chapel in order that his tenants might have the inestimable benefit of hearing the true Gospel preached in all its simplicity and power. He therefore built Ruxton Chapel at his own expense – which apparently caused a rift with the nearby beneficed parson at Marstow! Dying before the building was entirely completed, his son, the Revd John Jones of Langstone Court, determined that he would finish what his father had begun. At the time Mr Jones was not a Dissenter, and had indeed received episcopal ordination in the Church of England; but gradually, under the influence of some of the preachers at Ruxton, he became more serious minded and more evangelical in his views, until finally he retired from the Anglican Church and took up the pastorship of Ruxton Chapel. There he continued to make use of the Book of Common Prayer, but without being, as the record says, 'slavishly confined to it'. Later he purchased Langrove Cottage with several acres of land attached to it, which he left to trust for the support of his successors in the ministry, adding on a large room which was used for public worship and eventually became known as Langrove Congregational Church. He died in 1852, after having suffered several paralytic strokes which prevented him from attending worship as regularly as in former years, but to the end his attitude was so gentle, calm and patient that he was an example to all who had for so long been his flock. The building continued to be used as a Nonconformist Chapel until the beginning of this century, and many still remember the days when people trudged on foot from miles around to attend its services, or came on horseback or in pony-traps, the flickering lights of their lanterns visible a great way off as they made their way homewards even in the darkest and coldest weather.

In the garden outside, neatly framed by trim lawns, lie several gravestones, and the pieces of the large marble monument of the Jones family have been preserved and carefully pieced together by recent owners. Somewhere under the front doorway is the Jones family vault where some of the family, and the children who died young, are buried. They could not rest in a happier, more home-like spot. The whole place lies bathed in the day-long sunshine which its southerly aspect commands, and a more serene spot in which to have a cemetary-cum-garden, or a more delightful atmosphere of gentle happiness and peace, can hardly be imagined.

Only a few yards further on up the hill, tucked away so that it is scarcely noticeable behind its hedge and cluster of trees, lies RUXTON COURT, a little gem of a typical English farmhouse built up through the centuries.

A long, low, two-storeyed building, half-timbered at one end, stone-built at the further end, its central feature is the big half-timbered gabled porch standing out some ten feet from the ancient, black front door. The timbers of the porch are shaped to form a low, almost pointed arch, and inside benches line the two walls. The porch timbers have ornamental carved supports for the overhanging storeys which make the porch so impressive a feature of the house. It was here, in one of the bedrooms of this porch, that only a few years ago a sliding panel was discovered revealing a priest's hole which had been lost and forgotten through the years.

In the old, central part of the building, to the left of the porch, is the Elizabethan portion, the hall or main Living-room thickly forested with blackened ceiling beams which frown sternly down on one with all the serious gravity of their great age. To the right of the porch, in the seventeenth-century stone-built portion, there are small, single-light mullioned windows, some of which are blocked up and form alcove cupboards in the room inside. This room runs the full width of the house and still has its massive beams across the ceiling. At its far end, looking out over the field towards Trewen, are lovely old mullioned windows, taller and more graceful than those in the front part of the building, which looked out originally on to a cobbled courtyard. The old Elizabethan cobbles are still there, but now hidden under grass. Beside the gate, fixed to the wall, is a fine old fireback dated 1635, flanked by the initials M.P.V. This was dug up in the orchard some twenty years ago, and the owner decided it might as well be on view once-more. It is an odd reflection on the unpredictability of human nature that what we regard as almost priceless today was, not so long ago, thrown out as unwanted junk. Perhaps it has been like this through all the centuries.

Llangarron is 'the church on the Garron', that deep-cut brook which wanders through the hills hereabouts; and here at Llangarron we find LANGSTONE COURT, which has the entirely deserved reputation of being the loveliest house of its date and style in the county. Dipping down the Garron hill you come on it unexpectedly, catching a glimpse of old mellowed red-brick, half hidden by the trees. Then, as you cross the little bridge over the Garron Brook and begin the upward climb, you can see it in all its gracious, old-world beauty, looking out over its formal garden and the sloping green fields of its many-treed parkland.

The *Oxford Dictionary of English Place Names* gives the meaning of Langstone as 'the long-stone', or 'menhir'. But the present owner, Mr Colin Jones, feels that this is incorrect and perhaps a little fanciful. Nothing remotely like menhirs, or standing stones, has ever been found in the area, and there is no folk memory of anything of the kind. He believes it to be more simple and factual, being named from the long spur or rock which stands out here, and is only a foot or so below the surface of the soil in some places so that ploughs often drive into it when least expected.

Langstone Court itself is late seventeenth-century, of red-brick, with two storeys, cellars and attics. The roof is of blue Welsh slate, hipped, and with two gabled dormers, though the roof of the coach-house, set charmingly to one side of the entrance gates, is of the more restful Presilly tiles. The garden, rising from the early eighteenth-century gatepiers with their elegantly simple wrought-iron over-throw, has formal lawns and borders.

The doorway has a moulded surround, probably *c.* 1700, but the hood has been added at a later date. The stable block, running along the east side of the green, is also of brick with stone dressing. It is a charming little building with a central clock-turret, and also dates from *c.* 1700.

Beside the house, and behind it, extends the far earlier stone building which has indications of manorial status, though records mention it as a farmhouse. For the present Langstone Court was, in fact, added on to the older building, and gave it a new frontage more in keeping with the latest up-to-date styles of the time, and the civic status of its then owner.

Like all old houses which have been added to and enlarged and demolished, which have learned to sprawl comfortably over their green gardens, taking a bit here and giving back a bit there, Langstone Court is all the more interesting when its history is examined. Only two families have owned it since Elizabethan days, the Gwillims, and then the Joneses, who still own it, having bought it in 1794. Today the house is divided into two separate parts, Langstone Court being the seventeenth-century red-brick house looking out over its surrounding parkland, and Langstone Farm being the older, stone building at the back. If the *R.C.H.M.* is correct in dating Langstone Court as *c.* 1700, the builder must have been William Gwillim the younger, who inherited the property in 1698, and died in 1706 at the age of 55. The story goes that William, whose mother had been one of the Hoskyns of Bernithan, decided that he would like something in the same, modern style as the newly rebuilt Bernithan, instead of what was probably then his typical timber-framed Herefordshire farmhouse. Since even in those days building was not cheap, he decided that rather than begin entirely afresh, he would merely add a new frontage. It was certainly a very happy conceit for all concerned, since we have been left with the interest of the old, original house, and the added beauty, in a completely different style, of the new one.

Inside, Langstone Court has the typical hall-and-parlour arrangement of the era, still medieval in concept, with the Hall, which was also the dining-room, leading off into the Parlour on the left, a remnant of the hall-and-solar arrangement. Both rooms are lined with late seventeenth-century panelling, reposeful in their shining, restrained simplicity, and both have very fine plaster ceilings. These are more conservative than those of many of the larger houses of the period in the treatment of their fruit and foliage wreaths and other formal representations, which have a grace and elegance often lacking in the more effulgent displays of a later period. The one in the Parlour is particularly interesting, with its deep pendant bosses at the four corners of the centre-piece, and surrounded by a deep arabesqued border. One of the Jones family (who were, for the most part, clergy) had the inspired idea of lengthening the windows on the ground floor, which not only increases the light in the room, but affords a wonderful view over the surrounding countryside. It also adds greatly to the effect of graciousness and dignity given by the house, since the slender glazing bars of the long sash-windows give a generally lighter and more sophisticated appearance than did the transomed windows shown in old illustrations of the house in the mid-1700s.

Beyond the Hall and Parlour lie the two staircases (one older by far than the modern frontage of the house) and the older rooms of the building. The middle part of the south wing, which was built in the early 16th century, incorporates a cruck-truss, possibly of a far earlier date. One of the rooms has been transformed by a large bow-shaped addition built on *c.* 1825, when the Revd John Jones decided that a larger dining-room was called for adequately to seat his increasing family. Now the Drawing-room, it is a lovely room, high-ceilinged, light and sunny, with its long, elegant bow windows leading out into the garden. Two columns (of wood, skillfully disguised to look like stone) mark the place where the large bow begins, its weight carried by a hidden beam in the ceiling above, and give a touch of formal dignity and grandeur which would have been lost had the room ended merely in a simple bay.

Both the staircases are interesting, the first one built in well form, with dark, oak, turned balusters and panelled newells. The second staircase is probably early seventeenth-century, with lovely flat, shaped balusters diminishing in height on the upper floors, and moulded rails with square newells and tall moulded terminals. The soffits of the stairway ceilings also have oval plaster panelling. All through the house there is the gleam of old, dark oak, polished by use and age to a deep satiny sheen, set against the white plasterwork of ceilings and those walls which are unpanelled.

In such a house there are always chances of surprise when repair work is undertaken. The original wattle and daub of the older walls sometimes comes to to the surface unexpectedly, or the timber fronting may be exposed, as on the wall which must have been the old frontage of the house, now beside the front staircase. Unfortunately no hidden treasure has come to light, but a George III shilling was once found under the floorboards, and a puzzling, and quite literal, skeleton-in-the-cupboard was discovered some years ago when a wall was being taken down by the old staircase. Behind it was a small room, not much more than a large cupboard, and in it was the skeleton of a man sitting at a table with a pack of Elizabethan playing-cards in front of him, and an Elizabethan shilling-piece, still in possession of the family. In his head was a bullet-hole, and by his hand lay a pistol . . . If only we knew the story behind this little tragedy! Had he perhaps gambled away his inheritance and taken the only way out which he could see remained to him? Was that the reason why Langstone was sold and came into the possession of the Gwillim family? But why was the luckless man bricked up in the little cell where he had taken his life, instead of being buried in the usual way? We shall never know the answer, but it holds the germ of a great novel with its sense of mystery and sadness, of tragedy and despair . . .

LANGSTONE FARM, the adjoining, older building, is full of its own interest. No record exists as to when it was first built, but it has obviously had many additions through the years. It bristles with cruck-trusses, and the back wall of the farm Living-room has timber framing and was part of the original house. The dating of crucks is gradually being pushed back and back in time, but wherever we place it, the oldest part of Langstone is very old indeed. Recently repairs were done to the blades of a cruck and some other work was undertaken at the same time. Carved beam-ends were revealed, indicating that at one time there was an overhanging storey here on what must have been an external wall.

A former owner, Mr Harry Amos, told me of the consternation caused when a floor in the Kitchen was renewed and suddenly the centre collapsed, revealing an old, and very deep well. It must once have been in the courtyard of the house until the building was enlarged and the well covered up – obviously long before planning permission had to be obtained for work done in 'the Englishman's castle'! An old storeroom, too, had the style of carvings on the beams which indicated that once it had been a living-room centuries before, probably in the oldest, original house.

A mile or so away is BERNITHAN COURT, believed to stand on the site of an earlier building destroyed by fire. It was built by William Hoskyns, who was born in 1608 and probably built Bernithan about 1690 or so. A barn bears the date 1695.

Tradition says that Langstone and Bernithan were designed and built by the same builder, but Bernithan was a completely new house, built on the foundations and cellars of the older house, whereas Langstone was added on to the older building, thus enlarging it and presenting a new face to the world. The two buildings are certainly very similar in many ways, though Bernithan shines white and square in the sunlight while Langstone is warm red-brick. The original entrance is now the side of the house looking on to the gardens, and the new drive comes in from the opposite direction. The old frontage is almost identical with that of Langstone, except that it still has wooden cross-windows instead of the slimmer lines of those at Langstone. There are five bays and two storeys, and a steep hipped and slightly belled roof of graceful line. The doorway here has a pediment almost identical with that at Langstone, but there is only one central dormer window in the roof, with two dormers to the sides of the building. It stands square, firm, an air of assurance and dignified ease about it which one might indeed expect of a house built by the great Hoskyns family. Immediately behind it, separated only by a rectangular walled courtyard, is another square building slightly smaller in size. This, however, houses the old kitchens, store rooms, dairy and other domestic offices, as well as the rooms for the staff in those far-off days when a house such as this was warm with the busy life of its own community.

Inside, the design of the rooms shows its affinity with Langstone. The original entrance was identical, leading directly into the large double room which was originally the dining-room, but now the Drawing-room, of the house. To the left lies the smaller room, once parlour, now Dining-room, whilst the door immediately opposite the front door leads out into the central Hall, as at Langstone. There is still a stone fireplace in the Drawing-room, a massive one which was probably a necessity because of the exposed position in which the house stands. The fine old staircase, again, is echoed by the one at Langstone, but here it is a left-handed one. Today the entrance lies beyond the staircase, opening out into the courtyard, and the big modern Kitchen makes life without the old array of staff simpler than it would be if it were still situated on the far side of the courtyard. The small, snug Study on the opposite side of the Hallway has painted white panelling still, a stuccoed ceiling, and a big stone fireplace with a massive old fireback. Originally this bore the coat-of-arms of the Hoskyns, but an arrangement was agreed whereby it was returned to the family and the present one put in its place instead.

Beyond the square white house of the domestic quarters lies a pond, and the barns and old farmhouse. On three sides the fields slope away gently, more precipitously on the fourth. Bernithan, 'the hill of the gorse', lies in a lovely situation in a lovely part of the country.

Following the signposts to St Weonards the road eventually slopes gently down from the great square stump of that old saint's church into one of Nature's basin-like secret places which, wooded over, centuries ago, would have been very secluded and out of the way. Cutting its path through the soil with restless, snake-like progress, and that fierce determination which is its peculiar hallmark, goes the little Garron Brook, charming in its summertime innocence but, the owner of Treago informed me, a veritable mountain torrent in bad winters, flooding and spreading with almost elemental fury. And down in the hollow, raised slightly on the side of the hill, stands TREAGO, sometimes called Treago Castle, but never, I am assured, a castle in the strict sense of the word – never, that is to say, a place built especially for defence, with barracks, court, authority over an area, and the responsibility to ensure peace and safety within those lands. Nor, indeed, would anyone sensibly build a castle in a hollow surrounded by hills. Rather, it was a fortified house, or *domus defensabilis*, a private home strongly built in order to sustain attack from marauders until such time as local troops could come to the rescue. Gillow Manor, already mentioned, is another example of this type of defensible home.

Treago would seem to have been built about 1475-95, at least in its present form, and it is believed that at one time it may have had a second wall around it, or possibly a walled enclosure below it; if this was so, nothing of it now remains.

Treago has been in the possession of the Mynors, so far as known records go, since early in the 15th century, though the family itself had been seated at Burghill at least as early as 1150. It is built in the form of a quadrangle, with four circular towers at the corners. But before we rush to proclaim identification with Norman castle forms, we must recall that to a very large extent this has always been the convenient style of building common to many races and ages. Even the humble Roman villa was built on a quadrangular plan, and in both hot and cold climates there is much to be said for such a style which protects from extremes of heat and cold and can house different offices and people in a small, close-knit community without much feeling of over-crowding. The courtyard here at Treago could never have been large enough to support the popular local legend that in times of attack the cattle were driven into it for safety. Had they been, none of the inhabitants would have had room to move or manoeuvre to ensure any sort of defence. It is more likely to have been a place where certain tasks could conveniently be undertaken in the open air, a meeting-place, a cross-roads, even, of those going from one part of the building to another. In the centre of it is a deep well.

For some reason the four towers are not all the same size, two of them being large enough to contain only a staircase leading to the upper floors. The top storey of the north-east tower is known as 'the pope's hole', and contains three small windows and a tiny fireplace – just enough to give a visiting priest a quiet, fairly safe place to stay in for a few days. Its windows afford good views of the road approaches, giving time for escape should any suspicious posse be seen making towards the house. The family were well-known recusants in an area strong in its Roman Catholic allegiance, and they were indeed in trouble for their loyalties at the time of the Gunpowder Plot, though they seem to have been restored to favour by the time of the Restoration.

The house has undergone many alterations through the years, floor levels, partitions, windows, doors, all being changed at one time or another; and the central courtyard has been roofed over and taken into the house itself, sometime about 1840. It now forms a most pleasant Hall with a fine Staircase twisting its way upstairs with the casual grace borne of centuries. Its present siting shows it off to good advantage. The windows on two sides of the house were altered between 1840–45 to suit the Gothic taste then prevailing. They look out on to the pleasant gardens of Treago, with lawns and lilly-pond lying serenely in the sheltered bowl of their setting. There is the peaceful, happy air about the place always pervading houses which have not known strife or desolation in any great measure, and portraits of past ancestors look down approvingly on the changes they have witnessed in their old home.

The stone, square, three-storeyed porch once led into the original great hall, now a large, convenient Kitchen. A little stone-flagged Scullery to the right has a plaster ceiling, probably mid-seventeenth-century, modest and unassuming in its simple rose and oak design (sure token of loyal allegiance), yet pleasant enough to indicate that this was probably once used as the parlour, the descendant of the original solar opening out of the great hall.

One tower – the largest, south-east one – has a strange over-hanging top storey. This was added *c.* 1770 for use as a smoking room – a room which would, incidentally, have magnificent views on all three sides. Inside, it is decorated in the Strawberry Hill style fashionable at the time, with a matching overmantel. When this was receiving minor repairs some years ago, it was discovered that behind it lay an original stone fireplace of *c.* 1480. Exciting though the discovery was, it was somewhat marred by the fact that at some time the stonework had been cut away leaving a large gap. Details were taken of the stonework and then the Strawberry Hill fireplace was carefully put back into place, more in keeping with its surrounding décor, having gracefully yielded up its secret at no cost to its own existence. Finds like this are always coming to light when renovations are undertaken in old houses; very seldom do they involve the treasure legend accredits to all old dwellings, more usually unexpected expense. Recently the whole of the roof has had to be stripped and re-slated, and, with provident prevision, it was insulated. At the same time the floors were insulated from the cellars, and the saving of heat loss in an old stone-built house has proved most welcome in these days of fuel problems. At the same time, behind the skirting board, the head of a fine, medieval open fireplace was discovered, reminding one of the many times the floor levels in this house have been changed.

Two mysteries indeed Treago houses, though not the ones usually accredited to it. The first concerns the portrait of a dark, black-clad lady traditionally said to have been the mistress of Treago when the Scottish troops were marauding in the area in 1645. She is said to have entertained them so royally that they were charmed into leaving the place untouched and her possessions unharmed. In the portrait her hand rested on a dark, mysterious handle, which viewers insisted was a sword-hilt, symbolising her courageous and martial spirit. History denies the legend, however, since the lady in question was dead at the time of her alleged exploit, and no future mistress of Treago was installed until her son married some years afterwards. Possibly some other lady in the area was responsible for the action, and the portrait gave a convenient handle on which to peg a name . . . a handle which, when the portrait was cleaned, turned out to be nothing more alarming than that of a black fan.

The other mystery is less easily solved, since it concerns an old fireback with Queen Elizabeth's personal coat-of-arms and initials on it. Why here? In her father's reign there might have been some reason for it, since the Mynors of the day held office at Court. During Elizabeth's day, however, the family had fallen on comparatively evil times, the husband having been killed, and only his young widow and three small children occupying the house, with no known influence or connections at Court. There is no 'Queen Elizabeth slept here' record in the family, let alone record of apartments perhaps specially furnished and reserved for her, or any anticipated visit. How, then, did the proud insignia of Elizabeth of England come to be here, in this area, at perhaps the most unlikely time of all in the Mynors fortunes?

Some distance away, so near the old Monmouthshire or Gwent border that the road wanders in and out between the two counties, lies KENTCHURCH COURT, hidden away in a dip between the hills. All round it stretches the park and woodlands where the fallow deer still roam at will. Exactly how long any house has stood here no one knows, but it is said that the older parts of the medieval tower are on Saxon foundations, with the rest of the buildings added on to it later. Scudamores have lived here for 800 years, so they and the house have grown up together, and know each other well.

The drive passes through the stable yard and then through a fourteenth-century archway, out into the forecourt of the house which, from this side, is long, *L*-shaped and crenellated. The steps from the Terrace-room and its garden lead down into the forecourt at the far end and form the shorter stroke of the *L*. The archways and buildings flanking it beyond the old archway and behind the south face, form part of the original fourteenth-century building. The house and tower, as we see it today, is, exteriorly, the work of John Nash and Thomas Tudor, but inside the tower the old rooms remain, as well as the narrow encircling stairway built in the thickness of the walls.

The first Scudamore recorded is Sir Allan, in 1091, but the first of whom we can with certainty say that he actually resided here, is Sir John Scudamore, who is described in a late fourteenth-century document as 'of Kentchurch'. It was this Sir John who married Alice, eldest daughter of Owen Glyndwr, and it was here in the rooms of the old stone tower that Owen Glyndwr lived out his last, melancholy years. Lady Patricia Scudamore assured me that it is not true that he 'hid' here in a secret room, since King Henry V made no attempt to capture the ageing rebel whose hopes had fallen away and who no longer constituted any threat to the throne. On the contrary, twice he sent offers of a free pardon which the old man stubbornly refused. (Perhaps, remembering the vicious act which had forced him to take action initially, he felt that the pardoning should have been on his side.) He lived on here, in seclusion, until he died; and it is believed though never proved that he was buried somewhere on the nearby estate of Monnington Straddel, where another daughter lived, and not at Monnington-on-Wye, which usually, and undeservedly, claims the honour.

The present Court retains some of the medieval features present before Nash redesigned this part of the house. A late-eighteenth-century sketch of Kentchurch shows us what it was like at that date. The arched porch with windows above, standing out from the Great Hall with its medieval windows, shows clearly enough where the heart of the house lay, and from it sprang other buildings of later date clustering around it, with hipped roofs to the left and right proclaiming their late-seventeenth-century or early-eighteenth-century descent. Behind is the old tower, roofed, and with nothing but its sturdy square form to indicate that it was in any way defensible.

The present porch, moved slightly to the left of its original position, leads into a vaulted Hall with a Study on the left. At the far end the Hall turns right into a long, broad Gallery lined with family portraits. Most of these were retrieved when the Holme Lacy estate was sold up so that both branches of the family are now sheltering amicably under one roof. Perhaps my favourite would be that of the fourth Earl of Chesterfield (who wrote the famous letters to his son), seen wearing an elegant grey velvet full-skirted coat and breeches.

To the right of the Gallery lie the Nash rooms, the first being the Dining-room which has a marble fireplace surmounted by a Grinling Gibbons carving of swags of fruit, realistic lobsters, shellfish and game birds, all forming a fine, flowing overmantel which frames the portrait, by Lely, of the second Viscount Scudamore. On the wall facing the window is a portrait of Sir Harford Jones Brydges, by Lawrence; probably much of the present structure and design of Kentchurch owes its origins to Sir Harford, who seems to have been of great assistance in guiding the taste and ideas of his young son-in-law.

Next to the Dining-room is the Drawing-room, with a fine late-eighteenth-century marble chimney-piece and a deep, heavily moulded cornice. Here, too, is a beautiful Gibbons overmantel, but this is unusual in that it has at some time been gilded, and one wonders what Gibbons would have thought about such treatment of his work. In the centre of the room is a fine, pendant, lustred candelabrum, and the rich blue-green brocade patterned paper makes a strong background for the furnishings and for the many family portraits which line the walls.

Beyond this, but not part of the original Nash plan (rather, a room which would seem to have been added at a later date to fill in the space between the Drawing-room and the Terrace-room on its high level), is the Library. This is entered through a low-ceilinged, narrow space (accounted for, I suspect, by the stairs which ascend above it to the first floor of the house) which opens out into the room proper under three Norman-style, carved arches, said to be copies of those in Kilpeck church, and supported by four columns clad with dark wood veneer. The ceiling in this room is lower than in the others since this part of the building is three-storeyed as against the other two storeys, but it is a very pleasant room, and over the mantelpiece, symbolising the Restoration of the Monarchy, is another Gibbons carving; this depicts an eagle holding a wreath in its beak, the pendant sides being of trophies and floral swags in pine, not in limewood or oak as are the others. It has a lightness and sense of liberty about it which is well in keeping with its theme.

Beyond the Library the Gallery ends in a broad flight of steps leading, under a high pseudo-fourteenth-century arch, to the Chapel Room, so called because of the huge ecclesiastical-type window which fills almost the whole of the far wall. Furnished with a refectory table and chairs, this is a room which holds much fascination through the portraits and sketches it contains. On the table are various prints of the house as it was in the past, and on the left hand wall is a full-length portrait of Sir James Scudamore of Holme Lacy in Elizabethan dress. It depicts him holding a lance and wearing a suit of field armour which is now in the Metropolitan Museum of New York. His plumed helmet lies behind him, and in a glade some way off can be seen his white horse.

Slightly to one side, and below him, hangs the portrait, by Edward Bower, of the last Viscount Scudamore, who was the leader of the Herefordshire Royalists. Slightly to one side of this hangs one of the loveliest of all the portraits in Kentchurch Court – a small wood panel in oils in an arched wooden frame. The National Gallery has dated it as *c.* 1400, and it is said to be of that Jack-of-Kent about whom so many stories are told, some good, some bad. The historic facts are that he was originally a stable boy from Cardiganshire. Sir John, noting his bright intellect, had him educated. He then acted as tutor to the children of the family, until Sir John finally sent him to Oxford, where he took his degree and was ordained. He returned to Kentchurch to be chaplain to the household and to teach the children, and then finally joined the Fransciscans, spending some time thereafter abroad. But eventually he returned, settling once more as tutor and chaplain, spending his time in writing Welsh poetry (mostly, I imagine, mystical) and translating the Bible into Welsh. For years a copy of his work was retained here at Kentchurch until it was lost or burned with other family papers during a long letting at the beginning of this century.

It is a beautiful portrait, the face of the old priest standing out clear and strong, much in the manner of Van Eyck, or one of the other Flemish painters, and, also in their style is the background showing Kentchurch Court as it was all those centuries ago. It is claimed to be the oldest painting of a country house in England. At one period the panel was sent to be cleaned, and the cleansing agent was left on all night, taking off most of the top coat of oils. I am not certain that this is really of any importance since it has left the delicate lines of the charcoal sketch showing through, adding greatly to the interest, and to the character, of the old man's face. It is a painting to be justly proud of here in this old house which, presumably, some Dutch or Flemish artist must once have visited. The mountainous crag behind, with its apparent fairy tale castle on top (which, on closer examination proves to be simply clever rock formation) might be supposed to represent Grosmont Castle nearby, but it is a far cry from reality, and far more in keeping with the castles of the Langudoc than those of Britain. Some artist who had travelled widely on the Continent, but worked in the Flemish style, must once have come here to Kentchurch and painted the old priest's portrait . . . but what a pity it is that we have no record of such a visit.

To the left of the Chapel Room is the entrance to the Tower, reached by a short flight of steps in the round turret built on by Nash. Through a wooden door in the panelled first-floor room the old staircase can still be reached, built in the thickness of the walls. Here the ceiling is moulded with lozenge-type interlaced work, and over the fireplace hangs the only known portrait of Owen Glyndwr, a sketch taken from his Seal. It shows a man of considerable dignity, sitting at ease, wearing a full-length flowing robe – perhaps the man of culture and learning which he was before false charges and seizure of his domains turned him into the indignant man of action and rebellion whose name still sounds like a clarion call in Welsh ears. For Owen Glyndwr was a fighter for justice, a freedom-fighter of his times, and originally his cause was just, even though he blackened his proud name by the vengeance he often extracted in the years to come. Perhaps, embittered by the long years of villification, and the memory of deeds he would rather not have had laid to his name, he lay here at the end in this square room, a man ultimately confused between right and wrong, necessity and excess, a man who held now only the remembrance of bitter, wasted years and lands. This was his room, and this is the room which he, or Jack-of-Kent, is supposed to haunt. More probably his only haunting is the evocation in our own minds of all he was and stood for, for the family all agree that neither of these men have ever been known to haunt the house at all. It is a pleasant room, though it must contain sad memories. What stories ignorance and superstition have built are certainly totally disconnected with either the mild, peaceable old priest, or the last great champion of Welsh independence against the English kings. Other tales of strange music and voices being heard in the cellars seem to be explained by a tunnel which was discovered in this century and appears to line up with one of those strange geological faults which frequently produce such sounds.

To the right of the Chapel Room lies the Terrace-room, built over cellars which were once the stables of the older house before a landslip altered the level on this side of the buildings and formed the high bank of the terraced garden. It is a lovely room, light and sunny, with windows on two sides. The large open fireplace has had a bolection moulded surround added to match the beautiful, gold-brown of the Gibbons overmantel and the two long panels of his exquisite fruit and flower work hanging down the walls between the windows on the opposite side of the room. French windows lead out on to the terrace, sheltered below the high wooded hills which give such an impression of peace, yet hide the elemental power they contain. For, apart from the earth-tremor in Elizabethan days, in 1959 a cloudburst sent water, logs, uprooted trees, and tons of earth and rock pouring down the hillside on to the old house, sweeping into it, smashing doors and windows and walls, tearing furniture from its rooms, strewing the courtyard and the land with debris – including parts of the priceless Gibbons carvings. The marks, four foot up the walls, still remain in parts of the rooms today. Books, family papers and records, old and valuable carpets, all were ruined; and furniture and doors (one of which was never found) were strewn outside in the courtyard and gardens in a scene of desolation which would surely have broken the hearts and courage of those who carry in their veins a lesser blood than that of the Glyndwr breed. It took literally years to put right the damage, to piece together again the lovely carvings and to dry out the age-old walls. But it has been achieved, and today Kentchurch Court stands there in the sunlight surveying the beauty of its setting, and remembering its historic past, reposeful and dignified as a grandmother who has known the challenge of the years, and known, also, that she could meet and surmount all that came.

9. **Sellarsbrooke Park**, one of the finest specimens of a family-type Georgian house in the county

10. **Sellarsbrooke Park**, the Drawing-room

11. **Sellarsbrooke Park**, Dining-room with unusual Wedgwood fire-surround

12. Langstone Court, built *c.* 1700 by William Gwillim, showing the bow-shaped addition of *c.* 1825

13. Bernithan Court, built by William Hoskins *c.* 1690, is thought to be the model on which Langstone Court was based

14. Ruxton House, originally a chapel built by the Revd Thomas Jones of Langstone Court for his tenants

15. Treago, showing the original fifteenth-century battlemented gateway and the eighteenth-century overhanging top storey of the old south-east tower

16. Kentchurch Court, where Owen Glyndwr lived out the last years of his life in the tower, now remodelled exteriorly by John Nash
17. Kentchurch Court, the Dining-room, showing the beautiful Grinling Gibbons overmantel which frames a portrait by Lely of the 2nd Viscount Scudamore

Chapter 4

ON THE BORDERS OF RADNORSHIRE

BEAUTIFULLY sited above the Wye, with lawns and gardens which slope gently down to greet its waters, is the OLD VICARAGE of Bredwardine, a pleasant early-nineteenth-century-house with canopied and pillared French doors opening on to its lawns. It is of particular interest to all lovers of *Kilvert's Diary*, that journal of the young clergyman who kept a diary for some nine years and recorded for us a vivid, detailed description of rural Victorian life in the area. There are sad and terrible passages in it, times of tragedy and heartbreak in the lives of the simple poor; but also there are pages of the most magnificent descriptive prose which sometimes almost spills over into poetry, descriptions of the countryside, and of sights and sounds all round, together with lively passages showing the life of the period as lived out on all social levels. It may be said to rank with the great diaries of English literature and is only less well known because it was discovered less than half a century ago, but to read it is a pleasure none should forego. The Revd Francis Kilvert died here at Bredwardine in 1879, a month after his marriage. He had been Vicar here for two years, and was dearly loved by his parishioners. He lies now in the churchyard near his one-time Vicarage. His description written on Quinquagesima Sunday, 1878, of the tombstones in the churchyard there 'looking like a crowd of men', is particularly beautiful when one realises how short a time before he too would lie there waiting for the Resurrection Morn.

The name, Bredwardine, with its pleasant, warm sound, means 'the village on the bank', and is derived from *brerd*, meaning the brim, or bank, and *wardine*, a homestead or village-clearing. The name is a perfect and still recognisable description of the situation, for it does indeed stand on the slope of a steep ridge which goes down to the river. Once there was a castle here and, indeed, one can imagine few places where it would have been a more necessary feature of the landscape, with the river marking the old, oft fought over borderland between England and Wales.

Across the river, but some distance away, lies the RHYDSPENCE INN. Perhaps an Inn cannot strictly be called a home (though many otherwise lonely souls might defend its right to such a title!), but it certainly is a house, a very public one in fact, and really the Rhydspence Inn has special claims to distinction. Apart from having the distinction of being 'the last [or first] inn in England', it has perhaps the even more interesting association of being one of the few drovers' inns, or houses, remaining on the old drovers' roads round here. Cattle were brought down from the north to the big market which was held at Hay-on-Wye, and in the big porch-room above the entrance there is a tiny peephole in the left-hand wall. This room is known as the Head Drovers' Room, and from here a look-out was kept for the first signs of the slow-moving herds coming down the steep lane leading to Rhydspence. The derivation of the name seemed obscure, though obviously connected with the Welsh *rhyd*, a ford. Other, varying, and not very satisfactory theories are sometimes offered about the rest of the meaning. Mr and Mrs Stephen Joyce, of The Cwmmau, gave me what I feel to be by far the most likely. The translation of the Welsh *spence*, or *sbens*, is 'a hole under the stairs', from which comes the archaic *spence*, or a larder or pantry, or place where provisions are kept. Therefore the name seems to be a lovely indication of the real meaning of this inn – 'the place by the ford where provisions are kept', or, derivatively, 'may be obtained'.

The date of the actual building is supposed to be 1350, and the porchway is said to have once been part of a manor-house which was finally brought here and added to the front of the house. It claims to be the oldest building in Herefordshire, a claim which I think could be strongly disputed; and also the oldest inn in the county, which may also be open to question. It may, however, be the oldest inn-*building* in Herefordshire, though there are probably inns which have had hostelries standing on their sites for longer.

Inside it there are massive beams, just as one would expect, and a lovely old open fireplace which keeps alive the whole atmosphere of a haven for the weary traveller on a stormy night.

Rhydspence lies at the foot of the steep Drovers' Lane which comes down from Brilley Mountain – not a true mountain, but certainly a high, windswept piece of upland. At Brilley itself I was surprised to be told that there was yet another Kilvertian connection in that it was at Pentre, the old farm near the church, that the diarist mentions that a Mrs Davies's daughter died at the age of seventeen on 22 July 1871. And whilst at The Pant Kilvert records that there is a boundary notch in the chimney which indicates where the boundary runs between England and Wales, so that in one corner of the room you are in England, whilst in the opposite you are in Wales – described under his entry of 18 November 1870.

Brilley was called Brunley in Saxon times – 'the dark upland pasture' or, as some prefer, 'the place cleared by burning' which, visually, is the same picture; in Norman times it was known as Brynlegh and for many years much of the land was owned by the monks of Llanthony. Some of the place names here indicate an early British Church on the spot, and possibly a British martyr, since we find Llanbedyr, or 'Church of St Peter', Little Merthyr, or 'little martyr', and a group of five cottages and an old well in the wood. A long, twisting lane, apparently on a ley-line, is called Apostles Lane, and along it there are old, old farms and indications of more life in the area once than there is today.

At the further end is APOSTLES FARM, a partly timber-framed house of which the middle part is medieval, with two crucks incorporated in the partitioning. In the 17th century an upper floor was inserted and wing additions were built. The upper story at the north end of the cross wing has two beams running parallel with each other across the gable, making an unusual and pleasant decorative effect. It is believed to lie on the site of a much older building, and I suspect that the many ecclesiatical links of the area may tie up with the tradition of the British church and martyr. The apostle links may come not so much from the legend of St Peter and St Paul so strongly held in these parts, as from the simpler mission -- of apostles, or 'those who are sent', coming to this spot and making a small settlement somewhere along the old track, preaching at the Cross, or crossroads where the two old ways crossed, running approximately north-south and east-west. And some time along the years one of the monks, or a priest, may have been murdered, thus becoming known as 'the little martyr'.

CROSS FARM is said traditionally to be where the cross stood, a preaching cross in local legend, but it was very unlikely that this ever in fact existed. What is quite likely though, in the context of the times, is that here at the crossroads the missioners or apostles might have set up their small hut to shelter travellers, one of their number living here and preaching to those who came. This may have been the origin of the old farm standing there today which, though interesting in itself, is of medieval origin and would certainly not date from those much earlier days.

But that there was a larger community of some sort living somewhere here, whether secular or sacred, I am more and more convinced. Perhaps it was at the old farm known as TOTHILL, way off the beaten track, down a long, bumpy path, that I began to feel most certain of it all. Tothill is meant to derive from *Tothulle*, or 'the look-out hill', and in this part of the county we find a number of *tuts*, or small hillocks, often associated with small castles once built on them. Small castles they may sometimes have been, but more often mere look-out forts or outposts. There is also the possibility that it derives from *Tytwl*, meaning 'the broken house'.

As I drove into the farmyard I noticed, to the left, a long, very old, immense stone barn, dilapidated but extremely large. On the right was the house, which had until recently been occupied by a labourer's family and was little more than a two-up, two-down building. Certainly, externally, it did not look very promising either as regards age or interest, but the vast old barn opposite haunted me as I went into the house. There, the new owners were undertaking many repairs and renovations – essential, for the most part, if the house is to be made really habitable again. They told me of various old beams, and we discussed the ghost which is said to live in an upstairs cupboard ever since it was chased there at the beginning of this century by an irate father. It had given no hint of its presence to the new owners, though their farm hand preferred not to sleep on the premises! Then they mentioned some old panelling beside the staircase, and we went to look at it. Surprisingly, for a house of this size and type, it went up two floors, and had carved decorations at the top. Quite clearly it was all that remained of the original panelling of an old, two-storeyed great hall of some dim and distant age. The rest had gone, but by some strange chance this had been preserved, still *in situ*. We began discussing the whole matter, and I said I had the feeling that there had once been something else here, something bigger and greater than meets the eye today. The big barn worried me . . . and the name, Tothill . . . and other things, too. No small Welsh hill farmer, busy struggling to keep body and soul together, would have had the time, labour, or need, let alone the sense of vision, to build a barn of these dimensions. I was told that inside it had very old timbers and crucks, but there was snow on the ground and it was growing dark; I could not easily have got to it nor seen much if I had. The exterior size was sufficient in itself to make me entirely certain that it had once been the barn of a much greater farm, manor, or community, than had existed here for many centuries. And then, the name . . .

I asked if there were any signs of a mound, or *tut*, and was told that behind the barn there was a mound, but now it was so overgrown with trees and shrubs that it was difficult to be certain if it had ever had any sort of building on it. Nevertheless it looks out towards the old track that comes across the far-off hills and down to the Cross. It is, in fact, in just the right sort of positioning for a look-out. Discussing it further, I was told that there are indications that the foundations of the house were once considerably larger than the present building and seem to go out on two sides, almost like the arms of a courtyard. There are three deep, soundly-constructed wells, too – not one, with which most places have to be content. In fact, taken all together, and bearing its lonely situation in mind, and the extraordinarily good views it has westward across the surrounding country, it seemed more and more that there had once been a thriving habitattion here, though whether a community of monks, or the homestead, probably defensible, of some family of long ago, it is now impossible to determine. But the little, square-built Tothill Farm, which had earth floors, dank walls and falling masonry not long ago, has probably seen a different and fuller life than we can guess. In isolated places like this, when Welsh raiders caught the inhabitants unawares and drove them and their stock off to the far hills, houses were left burned and half demolished. Since there were no towns near and their position was so remote from other habitations, it was a short step to decay and ruin, until men forgot that anything of any consequence had ever been there at all.

At the bottom of Apostles Lane, off a small, private road which winds through hedges and then out across a gorse-sprinkled common where sheep graze peacefully, are THE CWMMAU, and Fernhall, two lovely old farmhouses belonging to the National Trust.

The Cwmmau lies in a little dip in the hillside, just as its name, 'the dingles', implies. Though today the surrounding land is very largely pastoral and agricultural, there are still thick woods in places reminding us of the original, extensive forest here. Locally it is said that kings used to go boar-hunting here at The Cwmmau. I could not ascertain which kings specifically, but it is believed that the house was a hunting lodge long before it became a farm.

The present house probably stands on the site of an older one, but what is now the stable wing, projecting beside the old two-storeyed porch, is older than the dwelling-house itself. Inside, on some of the beams, there are coloured decorative markings indicating that it was a living room of some substance before it was used as a stable.

In earlier times the approach was up the hill to the large, square entrance porch which now faces out into the garden. This porch has oak seats on either side, and there is in it an interesting reminder of the way things were done in the grand style, in olden days. The threshold of the door can be lifted out, leaving a flat surface whereby horses could haul logs right up and into the house itself. Today the present entrance is on the other side, next to what were the old kitchens and domestic offices. The present occupant, Mrs Joyce, has made the flagstoned kitchen, with its two massive bake-ovens, into a small museum. Copperware and old kitchen utensils are on display, bringing back the flavour of life long ago. Visitors to the house find this small museum an added interest and delight.

The earliest records date back to *c.* 1700, when The Cwmmau was in the possession of one Thomas Welson, who married Sybil Mahollam and died here in 1720; it is interesting to note that both these surnames are the names of hamlets which still exist in the area.

In 1800 John Harris was the owner, and it was he who built Brilley School for the village. In 1850 the property devolved upon a relative, one James Bromage, a man who from all accounts seems to have had not only a very large family but also large ideas and a very strong personality. He believed that a farm should be a self-sufficing community, and everything needed or used by all members had to be made or produced on the farm itself. There are still cottages in Brilley, called The Spinners by the older inhabitants, where wool from sheeps' fleeces was spun to make clothing, blankets and other items needed for the household, and all furniture and agricultural equipment had to be made on the estate. His views would clearly have delighted William Morris.

The Bromages continued to live at The Cwmmau until 1920, when it was bought by a certain gentleman, a skinner and rabbit-catcher, whose name is a byword in the area because of his treatment of the old house and any other property he managed to acquire. He seems to have been one of the early forebears of that race of speculators who have stripped our land of her assets and sold the heritage of their forefathers for their own personal gain. The lovely seventeenth-century panelling was ripped out and, together with the original front door, with its iron studding and massive bolts, took Columbus's route across the sea for the sum of £3000. Then, since times were bad and the market for skins was depressed, he filled the house with fleeces and skins, piling them high in every room and cupboard, in every available inch of space, hoping to hoard them against the day when things would improve and he could sell them for a vast profit. When the house was sold it took years to get rid of the smell of mouldering and uncured skins.

Eventually, however, in 1930, a London insurance-broker, a Mr Menges, saw the beautiful old house, fell in love with it, and decided to spend the rest of his life restoring it to its former splendid state. Mr Menges was known as the Grand Old Man of Lloyds, and was indeed a grand old man in all his dealings. He was much loved and appreciated in the area, which became a second home to him and his wife. He died suddenly, and unexpectedly, in 1965, but by that time he had ensured that both The Cwmmau and Fernhall would be saved for the nation by giving them to the National Trust.

The present tenants, Mr and Mrs Stephen Joyce, put in electric light in 1971 and now, with central-heating and the good services of a large Aga, the house is bright, warm and cheerful even by modern standards. The rooms are light and flower filled, and the old oak furniture gleams as once, long ago, it must have gleamed under the ministrations of James Bromage's stern reign. Again it is a family home, filled with a sense of life and purpose, activity and cheerfulness.

The building itself is two-storeyed, with the cellars and outbuildings needed for a farm of this size. The plan is irregular, early-eighteenth-century for the most part, but with a late-seventeenth-century addition on the south-west. The widely spaced timber-framing is particularly neat and appealing, and the two-storeyed gabled porch is still a gem of the architecture of the period – even without the original door which the earlier speculator sold. (At least he forgot to sell the fine moulded frame in which it was set.)

To those interested in varieties of dovecotes, The Cwmmau offers a special feature, since its pigeon-loft is a most unusual one, running along the outer wall beside the front porch, above the windows of the sitting room, and under a small stone-tiled pent roof. There are about twelve nesting boxes tucked away in this charming little cote, so near the roof that the warm, gentle cooing makes part of the pattern of daily life.

Though the panelling of the bedrooms upstairs had been torn away from the walls, Mrs Menges and a sister determined that they would substitute something of value in at least one of the rooms; so the porch room has a fascinating mural running round the walls, depicting the story of The Fall and Expulsion from the Garden of Eden.

A short distance from The Cwmmau is FERNHALL FARM, parts of which date back to the 13th century. When Mr Menges bought this shortly after he had bought The Cwmmau, it had been used as three separate cottages for some time, but the original and oldest part of the house is the central portion of the block. This would initially have been one large single room, and the great oak crucks can still be seen together with other beams added during later centuries, even including our own, in fact. There is one extremely interesting truss with cusped braces up to the collarbeam; this has three-foiled openings above, which form two acorn-like objects below an elongated and rounded diamond. This might have been the old screens passage in a larger house, but it is a little puzzling here. Now, filled in with plaster, it forms the wall dividing the landing and the principal bedroom, and makes a most charming and decorative feature.

Sometime during the early 1600s another part of the house was built on. Interestingly, the manner of structure suggests that it was built up against the older house either to form an entirely separate dwelling or with the intention of pulling down the older part once the new one was built. Instead, an upstairs seems to have been added to the old, single floored house, and, later still, another part added to the other side, or far end, of this oldest portion.

It would appear that when The Cwmmau was built Fernhall was made into cottages, and the name seems to bear this out, since it is believed that Fernhall comes from 'farnall', or 'farmall', meaning 'the second farm' from the Welsh *fferm-ail.*

From time immemorial Fernhall has been in the possession of what, in other parts of England, would be called yeoman farmers – that proud, sturdy breed of men who were their own masters, never belonging to the feudal lords nor springing from the serfs, but maintaining a sturdy independence, wresting their own living from the soil, standing alone against the world, the weather, and all woes, and refusing to be called any man's servant, or to obey anything or anyone but the rightful laws of the country.

All this part of the county is full of interesting names, at first quaint and unusual. Nearly always, however, if their phonetic value is taken into account, and the sound rather than the spelling is broken down, it will be found that the actual name comes from a descriptive, and exactly accurate, origin. An instance of this is seen in the small cottage a little way along the lane to The Cwmmau, which is known as Amber's Lone. Broken phonetically into its separate parts, it eventually arrives at the Welsh *ar-byr-lôn*, meaning 'on a short lane', which is a perfect description of its situation. It is a fascinating study to trace the meaning behind many of the names on this Welsh borderland. BURNT HENGOED, not far away, manages to mix English and Welsh picturesquely – 'the burnt old timber house'. What was probably the old, original house before it was burned down hides itself away, with its memories, in the outbuildings attached to the present farm, and amongst old timbers and crucks there still remains one interesting beam with decorative marking on it – a reminder that once this was not just a barn or shed, but a home, a house where colour and woodwork added the touches of elegance we sometimes fail to appreciate existed in those far off times.

Further along the Kington road is one of the houses of the area which has had more than its share of mystery, history and legend attached to it. But it is perhaps best appreciated if approached from Kington itself. Coming on it that way, HERGEST COURT stands high, slightly forbidding and aloof, on the great mount which implies that there was once a fortified building here. Below, covered with ice and snow when first I saw it, is the large pond which is all that remains of the original encircling moat, most of which was still there when Robinson wrote his *Mansions and Manors of Herefordshire*. He rightly says that 'most of the architectural features were effaced on the Court's conversion into a farm-house', probably around 1750.

The house was the seat of the great Vaughan family, and is thought to have been built *c.* 1430 on the site of an earlier building. The Welsh bard, Lewis Glyn Cothi, describes it as having 'eight strong buildings'; and a print at St Fagan's, Cardiff, also mentions 'eight halls'. Somewhere around the middle of the 18th century the more dilapidated ranges were demolished, leaving an *L*-shaped range, and it is this which we see today, the short stroke of the *L* being of closely-set timber framing. The longer arm, facing north-east, is of stone, stern and unembellished, and giving a somewhat forbidding aspect from the Kington approach. Driving up towards the house, past the extensive range of farm buildings, there is on the left a smallish, sturdily-built building, now used as a barn and storehouse, which has an old, arched doorway and one remaining small, pointed, single-light window on an upper floor, betraying its antiquity. It has been suggested that it was a chapel but I would be surprised if this were so since there seems to be no trace of any monastery ever being attached to the spot, and it is far too large for a chapel attached to the house or castle. Apart from that, however, it is not set east, as would have been the case in usual circumstances for any chapel of the period, and it is entirely detached from the house itself, which would again have been unusual at that time. The indication of an upper floor also makes the chapel theory a little unsatisfactory. If it is not one of the 'eight strong buildings', I would suggest it was possibly the original old manor, a strong, sturdily-built, smallish hall-type defensible building, and that the enlarged court was probably built in the 1400s, as records indicate, when opportunity, and perhaps finances, offered. The newer building would then probably have been what is now the stone wing of the house. This would appear to have been the usual type of great hall, facing out on to a courtyard. At one time murals were found on the walls but were, unfortunately, boarded over. Inside there are old beams and trusses, and in what is now the Living-room is a massive old stone fireplace with moulded jambs and a four-centred head. Above it is a moulded shelf which has clearly been added later; and a stone head with a serpent coiled around the neck (part of the Vaughan coat-of-arms) surveys the room it has known so long. Outside, in an angle between the two wings, is a stone-built projection with a doorway in it which has a two-centred head and chamfered jambs.

In the later south-west wing there is a considerable amount of panelling, and a fine early-seventeenth-century staircase. The interior matches well with the much-timbered exterior, which faces on to the road and is reflected in the remains of the old moat far below.

There are many tales told of Hergest Court, of secret chambers and passages, of ghosts and nights of terror spent there. Secret rooms, small, windowless places where a man might indeed hide in times of danger, have been found. But those who live there today find it peaceful enough.

Entirely different in style, character, and history, is UPPER HOUSE FARM, at Eardisley. Lying on the outskirts of Eardisley, just before the Mountie Inn, with only a small part of its exterior visible from the road, Upper House is a fine and most interesting example of a half-timbered building, with an overhanging upper storey over-looking the road. In the side wall are two slightly projecting mullioned windows, one of them being at the foot of the stairway in the staircase angle of the house. What little is known both of its history and its architectural features is of great interest. Parts of the building date from the 14th century, and additions and alterations were made in the 16th century. Built on a stone foundation, and *L*-shaped, the main part of the house is finished in black and white, with stone tiled roof. On the roadway side, a short flight of steps leads up to a wooden porch, and once there was a huge iron-studded oak door here. Particularly interesting is the decorative effect of the large, round, black wooden balls which appear to be pendant from the overhanging storey here. These are, in fact, the ends of the upright beams which are hidden in the plaster and which, instead of having ended in the usual carved finials, have been formed into these large, almost cannon-ball-like shapes.

Every side of the house has different types of timbering, some closely set, some more widely spaced; the windows also vary from small leaded ones to the wider panes of later centuries. From the back of the house the full beauty of the original building can be seen, for big double doors, iron-studded and black with age, open out into the courtyard here, under a gabled and timbered upper storey. From the side of the house a window is pointed out in one of the small, projecting gables, as being the Coffin Window, belonging to the Coffin Room, to which we shall shortly come.

The entrance doorway of Upper House leads directly into what was clearly a medieval hall originally, with a polished oak, arched doorway and double doors on the far side of the building and in direct line with the present front door. Here there is a central roof-truss, with arched braces to a collar-beam, and the moulded jambs of a doorway in what would have been the former screens passage. The ceiling beams and wooden uprights all around are dark with age, and French doors now lead out into what was once the tennis court and is now the garden. On the left of the old medieval hall is the Drawing-room with its lovely polished floor and white marble fireplaces, but no ceiling beams – though there may well be some hidden under the plaster of the ceiling. Beyond the Dining-room, which has an open beam ceiling, parquet flooring and a carved and moulded doorhead, is the room leading into the north wing of the house, which houses the Kitchen and the great, shining oak staircase. The Kitchen has huge beams still fitted with iron hooks for hanging meat, and in its day could have housed an army, as the saying goes . . . and, indeed, as tradition says.

The beautiful old staircase leads up to a landing which still retains its centuries-old character, with polished oak doorframes and doors still fitted with their wrought-iron drop latches. On some of these there are marks of what are reputed to be battleaxes. In the principal bedroom there is still original panelling from floor to ceiling, the only other piece of the original panelling being on one of the walls of the central Hall. Above the bedrooms in this part of the house is the small attic room, coffin-shaped and with the small coffin-shaped window, which is known as the Coffin Room. According to what seems to be the most reliable tradition, this is where the monks who originally inhabited the house were laid out when they died, with a candle left burning in the window to indicate the spot. Once before, many years ago in Shropshire, I heard this same tradition – that whenever a person was lying-out in his coffin before burial, a light would be left burning in the window and the villagers and others would kneel outside the window praying for the repose of his soul. In this connection I was interested to hear, from a different source in the area, of an old man who had been dying in the Kington Infirmary several years before. It seemed that he could not 'die easy', and that something was troubling his mind. No one could understand what was worrying him so greatly, and all they could get out of him was that he 'could not die until he had lit the candles at The Apostles and The Cross' (the two farms mentioned earlier). He was an old man, nearly ninety years of age, and his confused and somewhat incoherent ramblings made no sense to those who nursed him and tried to comfort him. Perhaps here was an echo of an old, old tradition linking up with the lighted candle in a window so that all might pray for the departing soul, a type of ceremony more usual in Roman Catholic countries than here in England.

Also upstairs is what is still called the Chapel, a room with two niches in it, which is traditionally said to have been the small private chapel of the monk's house. Those who have lived in the house previously told me that a monk has several times been seen, wearing a brown habit and standing on the landing just outside this room. Less happily, in what was at one time the schoolroom of the house, is a large beam from which tradition says a man once hanged himself . . .

The tradition that Upper House Farm was originally in the possession of a religious order of monks, and was a rest house for guests and visiting members of their community until the Dissolution, when they were turned out, also suggests that in later times Cromwell lodged here and fed his men in its huge kitchen whilst he was besieging Eardisley Castle. Upper House Farm still owns a field called Cannon Ford Field, and local tradition insists that this is where the Parliamentarian forces forded the stream which fed the castle's three moats, and dragged their cannons across to a suitable spot which would give them a clear field of fire.

Tradition also ties Upper House up with THE HOLME, a fifteenth-century house only a short way down the main street, which is said to have been connected with the same monastic order and linked to Upper House by a secret underground passage. The belief that it was originally in monastic hands may well be supported by the beautiful, massive barge-boards over the northern side of the house. There is a strong ecclesiastical touch about the traceried work carved here which is reminiscent of church windows of the period. The north side of this house is of black and white and brickwork, but the side facing on to the main road is of stonework on the ground floor with modern roughcast above. At one time in the last century the house was used as a boys' school, founded by Mrs Perry Herrick, and run by the wife of the then Rector of the parish.

Eardisley is full of mysterious hints of a long, long history, far longer than books and church records indicate. There were two long-houses at the upper end, near Upper House Farm, though now converted into four separate houses, and half-timbered today, yet still giving a reminder of their original Welsh descent. Lower down the village, nearer the church and castle is another, also now converted into separate dwellings. Opposite Upper House also, but on the Woodseaves Road, is The Cruck House, a cottage in which the exposed end cruck may be clearly seen. Outside it stands the Pump House, a small, square building, ivy-covered now and with a stone-tiled roof, from which this end of the parish was once supplied with water. Further along the village, by the massive square-towered church, is a group of black and white houses, Castle Close, carefully and lovingly restored from the remnants of an old barn.

The old Castle of Eardisley stood west of the church, and today CASTLE FARM occupies part of its site. This is a pleasant, red-brick house with an apsed hood over the front door. Beside it lies the garden with the remains of the moat, now mostly filled in, but clearly definable. Mr Davies, the owner of Castle Farm, told me that once there were three moats at Eardisley; the ground is low and tends to flood easily, but Eardisley Castle stood here long ago regardless of, or possibly because of, the difficulties of access. For Eardisley Castle is meant to have been one of the earliest 'castles', or at least defensive houses, in England. In *Domesday* there are fifty castles mentioned, and two *domus defensabiles* in the whole of England. Of these, seven of the castles and both of the *domus defensabiles* were in Herefordshire, one of the fortified homes being this one at Eardisley. It was occupied by the Baskervilles from the time of the Conquest for five centuries, and it was here that the much detested Bishop of Hereford, Peter d'Aquablanca, was held prisoner in 1262 until his death about a year later. It is not entirely clear how the actual downfall of the Castle came about. Some accounts speak of Cromwell besieging it and battering its walls with his cannon fire, whilst others tell of a mob of Royalists from Hereford who came out and demolished it by fire. Probably both accounts are true and link up with each other. The family fortunes seem to have been in sad disarray at the time, and the Baskerville of the day was in his sixties and did not engage actively in the struggle. If Cromwell damaged the castle seriously, it may well be that the Royalist mob, ever on the lookout to cause trouble for those they felt were not supporting the King's cause sufficiently, found it an easy task to set it ablaze. Only one gatehouse is said to have survived, in which the last remaining direct heir lived, in comparative poverty, until his death in 1684.

Standing there on Castle Hill, Mr Davies told me how his father, a champion ploughman for the county, and winner of a splendid array of silver cups, had actually won the 1902 ploughing championship here at Castle Farm. He never thought that one day he would himself own it, as he did when the estate was sold just after the First War, and he was able to buy the house which stands on the spot where once the old *domus defensabilis* of Heredeslege stood.

Almost the proverbial stone's throw from the church in Almeley stands the MANOR HOUSE, warm with its old red-brick walls and silver-grey timbering. It is a picturesque old house, probably of medieval origin, but with additions *c.* 1500 to the east and to the porch. The west end was altered quite considerably in the 17th century. A short flight of steps between fine stone piers in the stone wall leads from the roadway up to the two-storeyed porch, with its gabled watch-room over it. There is herring-bone framing here and on the gable of the east wing, and the diagonal bracing gives a gracious finish to the whole frontage. The lobby leads into the Hall, and the Parlour, or Drawing-room, has a fine moulded oak-beamed ceiling which dates from *c.* 1500, divided into sixteen panels, whilst the fireplace has moulded stone jambs and an oak lintel over. Several of the rooms have exposed ceiling beams, and upstairs there is a blocked doorway, *c.* 1500, and a small ogee-headed lamp-niche, charming and unusual.

On the far side of the church, standing near the old motte, is CASTLE FROOME FARM, a black and white brick-filled timbered house with a stone-tiled roof. The porch canopy is stone-tiled, with carved and moulded supporting beams, and gives a touch of gentle elegance to the small, unpretentious house. In the white-washed stone wall is a big stone sporting a fleur-de-lys carving, probably brought, the owner believes, from a church or from the old castle. Inside the house are old beams and a stone fireplace. But to antiquarians and architects, unlikely though it may seem, the most exciting feature must be the great stone barn with wooden superstructure and corrugated iron roof which adjoins the house. It gives little indication of the secrets held within, or of the years it has stood there watching history pass by.

For this barn is of medieval origin, probably the former hall of the original house, with a cross-wing at the western end. The latest research on the subject has dated the oldest of the crucks inside from the 11th–13th centuries. The cruck furthest east would seem to be part of a fourteenth- or early-fifteenth-century extension. But to me, over and beyond the delight of the age-old timbers, the wattle and daub, the evidence of a central fireplace, were the pegs I could just see projecting from one massive cruck in a corner.

'Those pegs – are they square pegs in round holes?' I asked the owner. Turning to look at it, he nodded, almost casually.

'Oh yes, and plenty more,' he said, and led me over to several other timbers. There before my eyes was the evidence I had been seeking. Architects and antiquarians had shaken their heads when asked whether such things existed; no one seemed to have seen or heard of them, which was sad, since I had been told that the old saying came from the use of this method of pegging in old building and furniture-making techniques. A square, tapering peg, rammed well home into a round hole, was said to be the best possible fit, one which would never wear or budge. And here at last were great square pegs used in the structure of this age-old barn. When I explained all this to the owner of this unexpected treasure-house, he nodded. 'Oh, ay, it's often used in these parts. Some do say it's the best way to make a job last for ever. They do say that a square peg in a round hole will last from Doomsday to Judgment Day!'

Oddly enough, having found at last my Square Peg in a Round Hole, within the next few days I found several other examples, all in buildings of the earliest type of cruck, and all in more or less the same area of the county, that north-west corner of Herefordshire around Brilley and Presteigne.

A little outside Almeley proper is Almeley Wootton, and here, at the junction of the roads, stands the QUAKER MEETING HOUSE which was built in 1672. It upholds its Quaker heritage in its modest, charming style, being of one storey, with a half-hipped roof and black-and-white timbering. Behind it lies a small cemetery where the Friends lie sleeping peacefully in neat rows under their grassy counterpane, with small, curved, identical headstones stating simply name and age. They were mostly very long-lived, possibly a tribute to the even tenor of their calm, disciplined way of life. I was reminded of another tiny Quaker cemetery where not even names are mentioned, only a simple statement of fact: 'Known Unto God', written on each headstone. Perhaps a Quaker Meeting House could not strictly be called a home, but it certainly is a house, and for many who worshipped here it must often have seemed very home-like. For those who lie in the neat garden between clipped yews and massed drifts of snowdrops and daffodils, it is a Home of Rest until the Day of their eternal joy.

Glimpsed through the trees just beyond the Meeting House, lies a house with a lovely name – THE SUMMER HOUSE. Perhaps in other times it was known as *The Hafod*, the Welsh word for the homestead used in the summer where the family could enjoy the country air and the cattle could find fresh pasture. But even in English its name has a beautiful sound and brings with it the thought of long, golden, summer days of sunshine and the echoing sound of laughter mingled with birdsong. And for all of these its setting is ideal.

It lies high above the brook which cuts its way through the tangle of earth and shrubs that tumble down the steep hillside here, forming a small, private coombe, and is built of a mixture of stone, brick, and timber in charming disarray. The front stands back from the lane, and has a cobble-stoned courtyard. The rear has exposed timber-framing and three gables. At ground floor level the wall is mainly of stone, rising to brick and timber, and the latter has curved and cusped patterning in the square frames, giving a pleasing and unusual decorative effect which is repeated in the gable tips.

The south-west part of the house is believed to date from medieval times, with a central Hall open to the roof, and probably originally had cross wings at the south-west and north-east ends. Sometime during the first half of the 17th century the north-east wing was rebuilt. The Hall was divided into two storeys, and additions were made to the north-east and north-west sides, with a further addition to the latter being made still later in the same century.

Inside, the house maintains the promise of the exterior, with exposed ceiling beams in several rooms and a panelled cupboard in one room bearing the initials R.P., said to be for Robert Prichard who died here in 1679. Part of the blade of one of the original crucks is still visible though the inserted flooring has prevented the full glory of the old beams from being seen properly. The roof has cruck trusses with ties, and one truss has a trefoil above the tie. Some cusped wind-braces still remain.

Outside Presteigne, only just on the Herefordshire side of the border, stands THE RODD, the house which took its name from the great la Rodd family who inhabited both the older, and the present, building. The manor was mentioned in *Domesday*, where it is indicated as having been laid waste at some earlier day by the constant warfare in the area. Originally it was called Bradleige and this name is still retained in one field and a cottage on the estate which is known as Bradley.

No definite date is known as to when the original house was built, but records show that it certainly dated back to Norman times, and one of the la Rodds was knighted by Richard Cœur de Lion in Palestine. The crest, three trefoils with a tail (indicating that he had been on one of the crusades which did actually reach the Holy Land), may still be seen carved on an old beam. An old deed of the time of Edward IV mentions 'William Rode de la Rode, fil. Johannis.' In the garden of The Rodd is a cottage known as Little Rodd, which has a cruck truss inside, making it older than The Rodd itself – two centuries older, in all probability, according to Lord Rennell.

The old, original Rodd had been a refuge for some of the army dispersed at the Battle of Mortimer's Cross, and though it cannot claim to have sheltered King Charles years later in his wanderings around these parts, it may well have been responsible for giving aid to his party. A little further up the road to Presteigne there is a lane which the country people of the district still call The King's Turning. Local tradition has it that King Charles galloped off down here on a horse which had been shod with shoes facing backwards, in an endeavour to throw off his pursuers. It may be recalled that pattens have been found for shoeing horses in the form of footmarks of small children, or of cows and other animals, all indicating the lengths to which a really ingenious smith could go to throw trackers off the scent of a fugitive. Though some may scoff, the story is strengthened by the fact that some miles away over the border in Shropshire, at New Invention, there is an old forge which claims to have been the place where this operation was performed.

Because of their loyalist sympathies, the Rodds were expropriated and went down to live in Devonshire, not returning to their old home until the Restoration. By then the house had a Crown tenant in possession, one who had obtained its tenure by somewhat dubious means, probably for services rendered to the Parliamentary forces in earlier times. Regrettably, the Parable of the Talents had obviously been omitted from his religious education, despite his allegiance to 'the Party of the Book', and the building was in a sadly dilapidated and neglected state. Naturally the Rodds sought to regain possession of their old home, but it was some time before this could be achieved and the former tenant dispossessed of his tenure. It is believed that the rebuilding of the present house had actually begun *c.* 1596, and the date 1628 is carved on a beam over the front door, whilst one fire-back is dated 1629, so undoubtedly the business of rebuilding had been a fairly slow procedure. In view of the intervening troubles we can appreciate that when the Rodd family returned once more to their home there was a good deal of rehabilitation work to be done, in all respects.

Like so many other houses in the country, The Rodd was built facing north, because of the prevailing superstition that if you faced south you caught plague. This meant of course that few of the living rooms in the house had any sunshine for any length of time. The Rennells have overcome this defect by converting a large wain close behind the back of the house into a most delightful Library-cum-Living-room. It is a room full of character. The wain, older than the house itself, was four-bayed, and the great dividing timbers rise to the high arched roof like young trees, with a wide gallery at one end, in the style of the old Minstrel's Gallery. Windows now fill what were once the great entrances through which wagons could be brought into the building and kept under cover, so the room is light and catches sunlight nearly all day through its east and south aspects. By a lucky chance a tall, elaborately carved late-sixteenth-century overmantle was discovered at a house-sale and saved from what must have seemed to it an ignominious fate; for it had been covered with several coats of paint, the topmost one being green, with a range of colours hidden away beneath it. Careful restoration has brought it back to its original state, and the wood is now a warm, mellowing brown, the smoke of the log fires and the ordinary processes of nature doing the slow, steady task which gives to old wood its beautiful, dark sheen.

Inside, most of the house is black and white, in order to offset the lack of sunshine of its north-facing aspect, and there are open fireplaces with great beams over. But there are also four panelled rooms, with stuccoed ceilings of the period, and the room on the projecting wing on the first floor has a particularly good overmantel of the same period as that in the Library.

With the exception of a very few years, Rodds have lived at The Rodd since Norman times, and when the present Lord Rennell bought it back again in recent years it was a home-coming in the fullest sense of the word. By a happy choice of associations, when a peerage devolved upon his father, the family had decided that it should commemmorate for all time the old French Huguenot connection with the Renells of Nantes. So the title stands as Rennell, whilst the family name is Rodd, a perfect combination, both linguistically and historically, of an ancient English lineage, a place which has taken its name from it, and a French line which found in both family and house a true haven and peace.

Further along the Border still, where Wales, Shropshire and Herefordshire seem to hold hands and cling together lovingly, is a tiny village whose name is great in the annals of Herefordshire history because of the nobility of mind and spirit of a family who lived, and still live, here.

Behind the tiny church at Brampton Bryan may be glimpsed the two round towers and grey stone walls of all that remains of Brampton Bryan Castle. The original castle was built by a de Brampton in the time of Henry I, but the earliest stone castle on the site was erected by Brian de Brampton sometime during the later years of the 12th century; what we see today is, in its oldest parts, probably those portions which were built later still, in the Edwardian era, and the popular ball-flower design of the period may be traced in several places above the arched windows.

From the de Bramptons the Castle passed by marriage to the Harleys, *c.* 1309, and it has been in their hands ever since. Its defence under Lady Brilliana Harley, in 1643, against the besieging Royalist forces, has already been referred to in the first part of this Trilogy, and certainly Lady Brilliana has a place in the third for her wholly charming and enlightening letters written to her son, 'deare Ned', and to her husband, Sir Robert Harley. Little need now be said of that period of its history save that, after her death, the castle was again beseiged, and this time its gallant defence was in vain. Not only the castle, but the Harley family, were ruined, with valuable books and furniture all destroyed, live-stock plundered and driven off, farm buildings wrecked and rent unpaid. The three young children were taken to Ludlow prison, where it is said they were baited like bears, and asked the ageless question of all centuries down to our own time, 'Where is now your God?'

One of the very lovely things about the whole tragic story is that when finally the War was over, the first thing to be rebuilt by the Harleys was not their own home, but the House of God, that tiny, very beautiful church which stands so short a distance from the ruined Castle. It is said that the fine hammerbeam roof of the church, and its twelve oak supports, came from the castle's ruined Banqueting Hall.

Somewhere about 1663 Sir Edward Harley decided it was time to make a more permanent home once more. Most of the remains we see today date from the time of the Black Prince, when castles were built for purpose, not for show, and looking at the massive masonry walls of the old building, and even at its Elizabethan additions, he must have realised the futility of hoping ever to restore his old home fully to its original state. So he built his new house, still calling it Brampton Bryan Castle, slightly to the south-west side of the old building. There is little record of what that house looked like, but it continued to be lived in for some eighty years or so until, about 1748, his descendant, another Edward, now fourth Earl of Oxford, decided on his marriage to build a new house. It is this red-brick Georgian building, now called BRAMPTON BRYAN HALL, which stands today beside the castle, surrounded by green lawns and trees. It seems likely that the original frontage was to the south, where there are seven bays with the three central ones projecting and pedimented in the style of the period. The present entrance is on the west side, which has five bays and a porch comprised of four Doric columns. Inside, the rooms have the spaciousness in height and proportion which makes Georgian houses so pleasant for both body and spirit to relax in. The tall sash windows let in plenty of sunshine, and the panelled shutters keep it at bay when necessary. The raised wooden panels of the doors are warm gold-brown, a delight of beautiful graining against the simplicity of the architravures and headings which give an august dignity to the style of this architectural era. At some time the staircase has been altered, and now, instead of winding its way round three sides of a hall, as was usual, it has been removed to the far north wall of the house, where it rises with what might be described as Victorian severity – straight up, and no nonsense about twists and turns! Slightly alien to the architectural styles around it, it nevertheless has great character.

Brampton Bryan Hall is a happy house. The sad tale of the past has been overcome; not forgotten, because there is too much of pride and courageous integrity in it ever to be brushed aside. But it has been accepted as part of the heritage of a great family, and worked in with all the other treasures of the years. Perhaps not least amongst these, of recent years, was the work of the present owner's grandfather, who inherited the estate in about 1872. With a determination and energy which would have delighted his Puritan forebears, and must have derived from then, he set about putting everything in order, from the greatest to the smallest item. He was an indefatigable builder and planner, and he turned the whole place into a model estate, building not only new and up-to-date barns and farm buildings, but also new dwellings for all the workers on the estate, laying out the grounds with an eye for beauty and an obvious love of fine trees and shrubs, and ensuring that the ruins of the castle be at least preserved and kept tidy.

Strangely perhaps this Harley married a Rodney, just as one of his predecessors, Anne Harley, of Berrington Hall, had once married a Rodney male; and so the two branches of the families became even more closely linked. His bride brought with her from Berrington Hall four of the guns which her ancestor, Admiral Lord Rodney, had captured from the Spaniards in the West Indies. Two of them still stand on the lawns beside the old castle, blue-green against the true green of the grass, their dates inscribed on them, ranging, originally, from 1754-56. Sadly, the other two went for salvage during the last war. Like bells, the four guns had names: *La Cruel* (the Cruel One); *La Sobervia* (the Proud One); *La Veloz* (the Swift One); and *La Tronante* (the Thundering One). Under each name was written, not quite in letters of fire, but in letters doubtless worked out in that element: *Ferdinand VI. D.G. Hispania Rex.* (Ferdinand VI. By the Grace of God, King of Spain); and then *Violati Fulmani Regis*, which may be translated as 'The Lightnings of an Outraged King'. In the house is another Rodney reminder, a large model of his flagship, made in ivory and bone by prisoners-of-war; and in the Library Lady Brilliana's portrait looks down approvingly, as if well pleased with her descendants and their works.

Today the present owner is consolidating the work on the original castle, trying to ensure that its open interior is kept in repair and, as accurately and carefully as possible, retaining the original features so that what remains shall not be lost, and a moment of history enshrined in the courage of one woman and her small band of retainers shall endure as an encouragement for others.

18. The Cwmmau, *c.* 1700, showing the two-storeyed porch through which horses once hauled logs right into the house itself

19. Fernhall Farm, the central part of which dates from the 13th century

20. Rhydspence Inn, an old drovers' inn, parts of which date from the mid 14th century

21. Fernhall Farm. Detail of three-foiled cusped brace of collar-beam

22. Upper House Farm. Detail of cannonball-shaped beam-ends

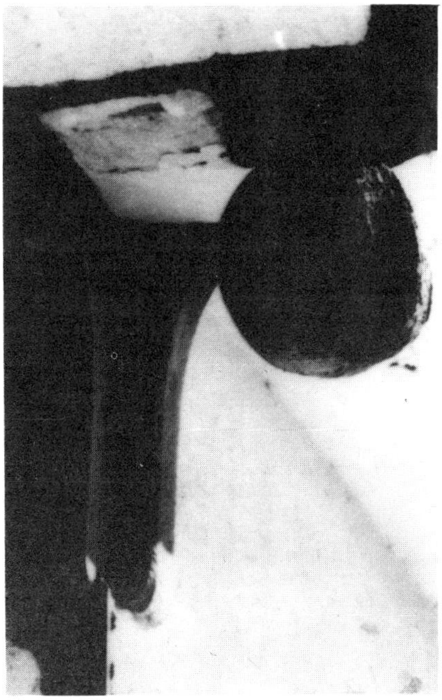

23. Hergest Court, forbidding and imposing, once the seat of the great Vaughan family and originally completely encircled by its moat

24. Upper House Farm. The rear view shows the full beauty of the original fourteenth-century building

25. Quaker Meeting House at Almeley Wootton. In its neat garden-cemetery the headstones state simply name and age

Chapter 5

KING OFFA'S COUNTRY

STRICTLY speaking, of course, HELLENS, at Much Marcle, should come before Ledbury and be included in the chapter dealing with the southern area of the county. But it is part of its strange history that it lies hidden, off the roads, seeking always a seclusion and anonymity which might safeguard it from passing troubles and enquiring posses. So now, as then, it tends to be left on one side. It is therefore more in keeping with its essential character and place in history that it should be by-passed, as it were, and only found unexpectedly. The sheer length of its history makes it impossible to include it with the southern area if that history is to be given any sort of recognition.

In its earliest days Hellens was just a small house built by a tiny community of monks serving the church they had built in the nearby hamlet. They built their house round the spring of fresh water which rose on a slight mound raised above the surrounding boggy ground. The three-quarter mile drive down to the church is still called The Monks' Walk, and somewhere below it a secret tunnel is said to exist.

Its life as a private house began somewhere about 1210, when the Lord de Balun was sent to police the area against the Welsh and the remnants of the old Saxon peoples who still secretly resisted the Norman authority. De Balun sent the monks off to neighbouring communities, and finally determined to build his castle on the little mound with the valuable spring of fresh water to hand. So the small monastery (and it was very small) gave way to the beginnings of a castle which was managed most efficiently for de Balun by his steward, one Helion. De Balun himself died before his new castle was completed, and his widow followed him shortly afterwards, in 1224. De Helion (we may note the addition of the *de* with interest) continued to manage the estate for the two sons – indeed, the de Helion family continued to manage it through more than a century, to their ultimate advantage and advancement, as we shall see. The younger de Balun, Walter, married Yseult Mortimer, sister of Roger Mortimer, or Black Mortimer as he was known, but died without heir in the late 1200s. After a decent interval Yseult married a friend of her brother's, one Hugh Audley. About the same time de Helion's son married an heiress from Yatton, called Agnes, which must have considerably improved their general and financial status – they had definitely moved up a step in the world, but continued as seneschals of Hellingham, or Ellingham Castle. The name itself is interesting, since it indicates that in the sourrounding area it was Helion who was the man to be reckoned with, not the de Balun lord, or the Audleys, and the new castle became known as 'Helion's place'. Through the centuries the name has changed in shape and style but never wavered from that first derivation.

The Audley family lived on at Hellens through the succeeding years. Even the aunt, the saintly Lady Katharine, lived there until her son died and she felt free at last to retire from the life of wordly society in which she had so little interest, and set off on her pilgrimage to live in a hermitage. It was not a very long pilgrimage, since she ended up at nearby Ledbury – but that is another story and has nothing to do with Hellens. Some of the land was sold off to the then seneschal de Helion; and the only child of Walter and Agnes de Helion, Joanna, married into the Walwyn, or Walwayne, family somewhere about the 1400s. Her son decided to renovate the old stone castle his family has tended for so long, and part of his work remains today. But it would be difficult to date or describe Hellens adequately. Its history, turbulent in its links with the great, arrogant Mortimers and the Crofts, and the little Princes who vanished so mysteriously from life in the Tower of London, knew more than enough of the life of the nation. Queen Mary Tudor knighted Richard Walwyn, who had supported her claim through the bitter treacheries of her sad life. Somewhere in the old house is Cavalier John Lingen's burial place – a secret grave, as for so many Cavaliers who had died from their wounds in the houses of their friends. Somewhere also is the secret grave of the old monk killed in the Queen's Room by Roundhead troopers before he could reach the hiding-place in the chimney of his upper-storey room, with its secret get-away that led through a maze of passages under the roof to the stables, a horse, and liberty. So intertwined with history and tragedy is it that a house like Hellens could hardly be ordinary in any sense of the word.

Down the Monk's Walk we come on the half-hidden entrance and huddle of red-brick and slate roofs which sprawls amongst the sheltering trees. To the left is a low, two-storeyed wing with a small four-pillared portico, fronting, somewhat unexpectedly, on to a forecourt with a fountain in it. Beside it, the house proper clusters round an inner courtyard, glimpsed through a low arch, over which the stone crest of the Audleys looks down on all-comers just as it has done for more than six centuries. The great black gates have handles on them to drag them open or closed – unusual handles, big, wrought-iron swags of laurel-like half-wreaths of a victor's crown. Under the low archway we enter the cobbled fore-court, sloping slightly downwards to the miscellany of red-brick which surrounds it, and the rather small door, still called Mortimer's Door, which is the present entrance to the house. It probably dates from the oldest part of the Audley buildings, incorporated now into the later Jacobean parts which have been built on to and around it. To the left is a low range with mullioned cross windows, and a massive old stone water-trough standing below them; to the right, an odd shaped turret juts out from the Jacobean range and mullioned windows which are all sizes and shapes, including a first floor one known as Hetty's Window.

From the east side, the house is calmer, more coherent in style and age, for here it has been built more 'all in one piece', and the big mullioned windows look out across lawns and the surrounding countryside. Here we can forget that what remains of Hellens is only a fragment of the old castle and its past glories. The Queen's Room, prepared for Queen Mary Tudor in 1554, looks out over the quiet garden. It still has the not entirely successful plastering above its fireplace depicting the royal coat-of-arms, supported by the lion of England and a surprised-looking Welsh wyvern, flanked by shields bearing the royal initials 'M.R.' The plumed four-poster bed with the red and yellow hangings of the colours of Spain still awaits the royal occupant who never arrived. It looks rather lonely now, standing beneath the new plaster ceiling made ready for the Queen's visit to the house she had known as a little girl long years before. From the centre of the unpretentious ribbed pattern hangs what is said to represent the Lily of France – a reminder of England's possessions in France. It is not a very good resemblance, but perhaps that hardly matters now, since before the unhappy monarch died the last of those possessions had been lost. Too much remembrance of its real meaning might be painful to bear.

It is this room which is said to be haunted, and there are too many strange incidents connected with it to refute the story entirely – like that of the young naval officer earlier this century who was invited for a week-end's shooting. All other rooms being already occupied, he was given the Queen's Room. He knew nothing of the history of the house, nor of the room in which he slept; but in any event he spent only one night in it and left the next day on the pretext, it later transpired, that he had been urgently recalled to his ship. Only years later, by a sheer coincidence, did the story come out. He had spent a very disturbed night, because, as he thought, 'some dotty old member of the family who had escaped from his keeper, had kept coming in and scuttling backwards and forwards between the north window and the door.' He was wearing some long, dark sort of dressing-gown with a hood. This was, in fact, an exact description of what happened to the murdered monk, who had tried to reach his secret hiding-place by going through the Queen's Room, only to find the far door flung open by a young Parliamentarian soldier. As he turned back to the east door by which he had entered, other Roundheads rushed in through it. Frantically he turned towards the great window, only to be mown down between the two groups and hacked to death. Today, caught in an eternal moment, he re-enacts those frantic, almost mindless moments endlessly.

In a room on the first floor, where the heavily-barred window looks out over the inner-courtyard, a mysterious women was locked in until her death, towards the end of the 17th century and the early part of the 18th. On the inside of the glass windowpane is scratched, with the diamond ring she wore, in two separate places: 'It is a part of virtue to abstain From what we love, if it shall prove our bane', and then 'Hetty Walwyn'. Nearby, on the outside of the glass, is written 'John Pearcel, 1702'. Poor Hetty! whose adventure into love was so speedily curtailed in stricture and in ultimate madness; and poor John! who came to claim his love too late. Was he able, climbing up to the window one dark night, pressing his face against the heavy bars, to explain to her what sad accident of fate had made him seem to have abandoned her, so that she came back home to face censure and the confines of this imprisoning room? Or was her mind by then too darkened by confusion and by grief to understand the message he sought to give? We may never know. The only evidence that he did come to seek her out lies in the signature he left cut on the windowpane.

Within the dark rooms of the oldest part of the house is the Black Prince's fireplace, above it a solidly built overmantel in stone with the Black Prince's three-feathered crest; and beneath it, in mis-spelt phonetic simplicity which authenticates it more than any neat correctitude, the words, *Ich deene*.

Oddly enough, one of the most touching signs to me of the passing years this old house has seen was the prosaic difference between the massive stone water-trough, with its carved stone head above it, in the inner-courtyard; the metal one by the outer archway, chased with classical figures and the inscription '1776 - G.H.'; and the utility twentieth-century version in the corner of the courtyard.

Flagged floors, black beams in the old Great Hall, dark polished floors, the musty smell of age and weariness which some old houses exude, as though exhaustion of their vitality was a living, almost tangible, reality – all these make up Hellens, the old castle-mansion which never thrived so well as under the stewardship of the de Helions, and on which some shadow seemed cast when the last of them died. The Walwyns brought their loyalty and their integrity to the house, but somewhere after the death of Mary Tudor a shadow seemed to descend on family and home, and perhaps the tragedies of the Civil War finished any chance of real light and ease returning to comfort the old building. It stands today, a little like its strange old ghostly monk, a building trapped in Time, not distinct in any one period, belonging to all yet to none. It is a strange house, with stories attached to it, and no one should miss the opportunity of reading *Hellens – A Herefordshire Mansion*, written by one who lived in it and knew it intimately, Malcolm Munthe.

Beyond Ledbury the country is flatter than in the central and western parts; seemingly emptier, save for the wooden gridwork which betrays the fact that we are in hop-country here. And even if it did not, then the conical hats of the hop-kilns would cry the fact aloud. Black-and-white cottages there are a-plenty, and the number of inns called The Oak, or The Royal Oak, seems to remind us that once the area was more afforested than it is now. The soil is rich. It is also one of the wettest and muddiest parts of the county, as one farmer told me on a particularly wet day, confirming my worst suspicions. Both facts are probably accounted for by its situation in the shadow of the great ridge of the Malverns which drain off their goodness and moisture on to the plains below.

At Bosbury, the massive, detached belfry stands up like a small fortress above its church and the black-and-white cottages which line the high street. Immediately opposite the church is a fifteenth-century hall-house, with its two gabled cross-wings surveying the scene it has known for so many centuries, and obviously musing on vanished glories. Just around the corner from the church is all that remains of the old palace of the Bishops of Hereford, in OLD COURT FARM. The massive gateway belonging to it still remains, entering nothing more majestic now than a farmyard. In 1630 the Bishops ceased to use the manor, or palace, and a few years later the main structure was demolished, but the gateway and a dovecote, said to have been built in the time of Edward I, were left. It is believed to have been one of the oldest of the manors belonging to the Bishopric, and the *Harleian Manuscript 6726* states that the Bishops 'held their State here and dwelt in a fayre palace in the time of King Offa.' At least two Bishops died here, one of them being the saintly Bishop Cantilupe, whose favourite residence it was said to be. The cider cellar is all that remains of the old refectory. Some fifty years ago plaster falling from the ceiling in this room revealed a carved ceiling which is believed to have been covered over during the Civil War.

Not far away is TEMPLE COURT FARM, once a preceptory of the ill-fated Knights Templars, but with little remaining today to remind the visitor of its past historical links.

At BOSBURY HOUSE white fantail doves make a purr of content from their loft above the stables of the courtyard, which is set to one side of, and slightly behind, the house itself. This latter is Georgian, with additions of 1873 or so. Brick-walled, it has stone dressings and is of two storeys with a dignified stone balustrated roof gracing it like a crown. There are seven bays in the main house, with a stone entrance porch on four Tuscan pillars, and five bays in the slightly lower addition on the left of the house. It is a home of great dignity and charm, and on the south side broad steps lead up from the gardens to a terrace with full-length windows opening out on to it, whilst at the back there is a small walled garden with a pedimented archway and a finely-wrought iron gate opening into it.

Inside, one room has a moulded ceiling with an unusual frieze of hops round it – the only one I know of apart from a similar design at Frogmore, near Weston-under-Penyard.

On a slight incline some distance along the road is HILL HOUSE FARM, an entirely different sort of building, being black-and-white, dating mostly from *c.* 1600, though it is believed originally to have been a hunting lodge earlier than that in the days when this was forest land. Square and narrow timber framings make a pleasant interplay of contrast enlivened in parts by concave lozenge-type framing. Under the present brickwork there is daub-and-wattle, and indications of the original dimensions before the further end was added on together with the much later hop-kiln, now disused.

Further on still, tucked away at Sutton St Nicholas, is a house where once the famous Backhouse Daffodils were first raised: SUTTON COURT, once the home of Col. Backhouse, so well known in the field of daffodil specialists. Clustered amongst sheltering trees and unusual shrubs, its red-brick eighteenth-century face is half hidden from the road; and its white-painted arched windows are sliced into thirds by horizontal sash-bars.

The present Kitchen is the big Court Room from which the house takes its name, and where once sentence was given and pleas for clemency heard. Today no more tragic cry is heard than the shrill whistle of the kettle, or the merry bubbling sounds of jam-making; but reminders of other days are there in the small windows, high up above the panelling, or in the tiny cell in the basement of the house. And beyond the formal garden and the large, red-brick walled garden, is a long avenue between beech hedges – once the archery butts to which the gentry came to practise their skills in previous centuries.

Just after leaving the Suttons, the road branches off towards Moreton-on-Lugg, and here at the roadside stands a reminder of a moment of tragedy enshrined today in beauty and serenity – a delightful brick-and-timbered little cottage with (unusual in this county) a thatched roof, standing on smooth lawns bordered with shrubs and flowers, so cool and calm it is incredible that it should ever have been conceived by stress and violent drama. Yet on a plaque on the wall is an inscription which reads: 'THE OLD SCHOOL HOUSE founded 1610 by Jane Shelley, widow of Wm. Shelley, who suffered for plot in favour of Mary Queen of Scots 1583.'

All we know of William Shelley for certain is that he came from Michaelgrove, in Sussex, and that he married Jane Lingen, one of the Lingen family of Herefordshire. The rest is conflicting evidence. One story says that he suffered execution with Francis Throckmorton, son of Sir John Throckmorton, who lived in nearby Marden. Another says that his only crime was that he petitioned Queen Elizabeth for a mitigation of the laws against the Roman Catholics because they had displayed so much loyalty to her at the time of the Spanish Armada. Another account, that given in the official records, is somewhat different and charges Shelley with 'having imagined and compassed the death of the Queen, the subversion of the established religion and government, and the procurement of an invasion of the kingdom.' Evidence given at his trial included a traitorous interview with outlaws and those in high quarters known to favour the Scots' Queen's cause. It would seem that he was found guilty, committed to the Tower, and sentenced to death. But whether that sentence was ever carried out is uncertain, since it appears that he ended his days in the Marshalsea prison, though how long after, or whether through sickness or other cause, is not mentioned. His wife Jane is said to have been cast into the common gaol in Worcester because she had sheltered a priest in her house.

Here we are in the area known as Paradise – probably originating, as Bannister suggests, in the 15th century when crops were grown from Paradise-seed imported from Morocco or Tripoli. Here is UPPER PARADISE FARM, an old black-and-white, brick-and-timbered building, not very exceptional externally, but housing an interesting plaster ceiling decorated with a pattern of leaves and men's heads. One of the heads wears a crown.

All this area is associated with the murder, up on Sutton Walls, in Offa's Palace, of King Ethelbert, *c.* 794. After Offa's scheming queen had drugged the young Saxon king's wine, one Gimbert, or Gunbertus, beheaded him with a sword. The somewhat grisley story says that Gimbert and his friends proceeded to play football with the king's head, down from the high scarps of Sutton Walls until, by the banks of the river, they tired of their sport and left it there. King Offa, in a fit of remorse-cum-neurosis, indicated his revulsion at this behaviour and ordered that the body be reunited with its missing member, and given burial. So the remains of the young king were buried by the river. Immediately things started to happen: Offa's daughter began to prophesy (accurately); his people began to mutter against him; and each night a strange light appeared over the martyr's grave. Eventually, under stern reproofs from Bishop Eadwulf, uttered publicly that all might know, and the pressure of public opinion thus stirred up, Offa ordered that the body be given proper burial at Hereford, and a shrine be built over it, at his own expense. Where the body had been buried, on the river banks, a spring sprang up. Today it is still there, right inside the parish church of Marden, a well which can be seen when the cover over it is lifted. The crowned head on the ceiling at Upper Paradise Farm is believed to represent this tradition, though some say it represents that later martyr king, Charles I, as some of the Marden families were strong Royalists.

Black-and-white timbered cottages abound, mostly of the late 17th and early 18th centuries, but perhaps of especial interest, though not a timbered building or of any particular beauty, is the Blacksmith's Forge near the Post Office and The Volunteer Inn. Three hundred years ago it was a forge, as it is today, though the present records go back only to 1856, when the great-grandfather of the present smith was smithing there then. It is believed to be one of the oldest forges still working in the country.

In the area known as The Vauld, lies an old farmhouse known by the same name. The word seems to come from the Old English *fald*, meaning a sheepfold, which is the first form in which it is recorded (in 1465), although these low-lying, marshy lands would seem a strange place to graze sheep. The other possibility is that it links up with the Old German *wald*, or wood, which may well be the case since there is reason to believe that the area was once wooded, mainly with willows, hazel, alder, and other trees which can endure having wet feet.

The VAULD FARM is a black-and-white timber-and-brick building dating from the 16th century, though parts of it may date from well before that. It is believed to have been mentioned in Domesday, though clearly this would not be the building we see at present. Nearby is Red Barn, belonging to the Vauld estate, also a brick-and-plaster timbered building. Inside the older part of it are crucks and old rafters with a beam dated 1620. The stone barn nearby dates from *c.* 1570. A red-brick oast house stands next to the house, reminding the world that this was once hop-growing land, whilst further up the lane is a small cottage called Vine Villa, probably a lingering memory of vineyards belonging to the old, nearby monastery at Amberley Court. The original house was probably built for the steward of the vineyards, and the name remains even though the house itself has long since gone.

A few yards away is HOPE LODGE, an old stone house with ecclesiastical-type windows, which featured in *The Survivors* television series. The original house was built *c.* 1750, and then had a chapel added to one side in brick. What had been a front room was extended, and had a balcony, or gallery, built above it until about 1953, when it was walled up, the chapel divided into two, and a new ceiling inserted. It was first a Methodist chapel, then used by the Salvation Army, and now the room is the Drawing-room of the house, retaining an atmosphere of peaceful happiness and light.

At Upper Maund is another example of a building built for another purpose becoming used as a house in our own day. The Maunde School, built *c.* 1860 (at the incredibly low cost of £569.19.6d.), was a stone schoolhouse with teacher's house attached – the simple solution to housing as well as transport problems in times past. Its life as a school, however, was short-lived, since it was closed down shortly after 1890 and pupils were then transported 'in the brake' (the equivalent of modern bussing, but sounding more dignified) to Bodenham School daily. Thereafter the little Maunde School was used for Sunday School and Sunday services, becoming known ultimately as the Maund Bryan Mission Hall. A glance at records of some of the payments is revealing by our standards:

Materials and fittings	*£468.—.—.*
Architect's fees	*37.19. 6.*
Labourers	*15.—.—.*
Gate	*4. 6. 6. etc.*

Fittings such as door handles and locks are beautiful, massively constructed in iron to last 100 years at least.

Now THE MISSION HALL at Maund Bryan is being painstakingly renovated. The long schoolroom with its high ceiling and lovely trinity of arched windows on three sides is to be the Studio, with good north lights and plenty of space and height. The schoolmistress's house, two up and two down, long neglected and drear, is being converted into a bright and pleasant family home. The outbuildings are being renewed and reconstructed to form workrooms and utility rooms, and, true to the country tradition of self-sufficiency, there is a shed and a stye for live-stock. Soon, with hens, geese, ducks and piglets making their homely sounds around the old stone building, the once half-derelict house will blossom into life again, knowing that peace and beauty which bred joy and contentment, and made for a sturdy independence in men's hearts through the centuries. It is hardly surprising that all around the county the same thing may be encountered – men and women who have bought up small, half-derelict places, and are themselves renovating them, laboriously, painstakingly, stone by stone often enough, having turned their backs on the slavery of industry and the rat-race of commerce, to seek again the life of their forefathers who would never allow themselves to be feather-bedded into a somnolence barely distinguishable from death. And to the communities they join, such people bring their own skills and abilities, helping to enrich that village life which was in danger of decaying through sheer depletion when men followed the deluding fire-fly which beckoned them with the allure of the big cities.

For antiquarians, AMBERLEY COURT must not be missed. The exterior gives little indication of just what treasure is housed within, half-hidden away now by the addition, three centuries ago, of an upper floor. For this is an almost perfect example of a fourteenth-century house with high central Hall and Solar and Buttery wings. The description given in the *R.C.H.M.* should be read, and the drawings studied, since they give the fine detail of this roof, with its rare type of construction, which cannot now be seen except in the attics. Apart from the added floor and ceiling, when the Hall was divided into two storeys, nothing has been added or destroyed since this roof was built six hundred years or more ago. Even the offending ceiling is a joy, with its chamfered beams three centuries old – it almost makes one forgive it for hiding the glories up above. A date on the beam in the house is 1452. Historians have disputed this, since the form of *4* used was not in fact in use until the 16th century. But, here as elsewhere, it is now felt that the date may have been added in at that time simply handing down a tradition – a sort of minor *Domesday* or *R.C.H.M.*, worked out *in situ*.

Across the farmyard is a little chapel, with parts dating from the early 14th century. A sketch of it dated 1862 shows it as a near ruin, but fortunately it has been well restored, and services are held there regularly during the summer just as they were, centuries ago, when it belonged to the old monastery of Amberley.

Much nearer the eastern border of the county is Whitbourne. But a tantalising glimpse is all one gains of WHITBOURNE HALL as one drives through the country lanes around it – and that is probably all its builder intended should be gained.

For Edward Bickerton Evans had made his way up the social scale by sheer hard work, in the vinegar and country-wine family business which his father had founded in Worcester with a partner. When he was about 40 years of age he decided that it was time for him to adopt the more comfortable stance of a country gentleman. The site he chose which would enable him to fulfil this ambition was indicative of his good business sense, for it was only ten miles from Worcester, yet set in an area of gently rolling wooded hills with long historical associations. For centuries the Manor of Whitbourne had belonged to the Bishop of Hereford, until the time of the Commonwealth, when it had been practically destroyed; it was then rebuilt, largely by Col. Birch, and after his death rented out to various farming families. Doubtless Edward Evans was disappointed that it was not on the market when he began buying up farms in the area, and so drew up plans for his own great house which was built between 1860-62.

Whitbourne Hall faces southwards, looking out over the valley, and it stands in the midst of the arboretum which Edward Evans carefully planned and built up. The house is built of light grey ashlar, which shines white in sunshine and yet has the coolness of the Classical tradition in which its fine entrance portico was designed. The front door opens into a narrow vestibule, similar in style to many houses of the era, and immediately facing the massive double entrance doors are other doors, equally impressive, with upper grilles of bronze. These in turn open into the Main Hall, a large room, 50ft by 40ft, with Grecian columns and a geometrically patterned tiled floor. At the far end of the Hall is the Main Staircase, which leads to a half-landing and then divides into two, to form galleries on either side of the Hall.

All the main rooms open directly out of the Hall. The Dining-room, still with its original furniture in place, is 40ft by 25ft, and has a black marble fireplace. The Library has a grey marble fireplace and access into the Dining-room as well as into the Hall. Perhaps the most distinctive room, in furnishing and in style, is the Drawing-room, where a great bay, 30ft wide and 10ft deep, enlivens the otherwise rectangular shape of most of the rooms. Here the fireplace is light grey and wall decorations are the original ones, featuring the Adam revival popular at the time but with obvious yearnings towards the Louis-Quatorze period.

One of the most intriguing features of the house is to be found in the door-furniture fittings of the Bedrooms, where ivory is used for the ladies' Bedrooms, ebony for the gentlemen's.

Also built in the Classical tradition is BERRINGTON HALL, lying further north in the county. It faces south-west, looking away over parkland laid out by Capability Brown towards the Black Mountains, with the green-brown hues of Radnor Forest lying due west.

Perhaps the front of the house gives little indication of the full scale and grandeur of the plan conceived in 1778–81 by Henry Holland for the Rt Hon. Thomas Harley, since it is a plain rectangular building, with the domestic offices lying beyond it. These form outlying wings round a courtyard which is larger than the house itself, with the Laundry, Drying Rooms, Bakery, Engine-room and Steward's Office forming the fourth side, through which entrance is obtained into the courtyard by a wide, pedimented archway. It is, in fact, far larger and more impressive inside than might appear at first sight. The inside is also more impressive than the original designs indicate, and this is probably to be accounted for by the marriage of Thomas Harley's daughter, Anne, with the son of the great Admiral Lord Rodney. Since Anne and her husband succeeded Thomas Harley here, it would seem that much of the grandeur inside, which is linked with the Rodney naval victories, was included for their benefit. One old engraving shows four ten-pounder Spanish naval guns standing on the lawns, but, as already described, these were removed to Brampton Bryan Hall when a later generation of Rodneys and Harleys decided to unite the families once again in marriage.

The house itself is of pink sandstone ashlar masonry, two-storeyed, with basements, and attics cunningly hidden behind a balustraded parapet. The portico gracing the front entrance is in the Classical style. Ionic columns support a full, deep entablature, but the proportions of the pillars somehow do not seem entirely right, possibly because the portico dominates and dwarfs the rest of the frontage. At one time the original pediment was replaced by a three-storeyed tower, totally out of keeping with the style, but under the National Trust the pediment has been restored. Originally this carried the Harley coat-of-arms, but the soft pink stone became defaced, and now a lunette window has replaced the carving.

The arched and panelled double doors seem slightly narrow against the rest of the portico, but at least they match the simplicity of Holland's preferences. They lead into the Marble Hall – where many may feel that Holland's desire for simplicity was misguidedly over-ruled. The central doorway here is recessed and pedimented, but the others have panels with material trophies over them which detract from, rather than add to, the dignity of the room with its black, white and variegated marbles.

The pedimented door leads into the Inner, or Staircase, Hall; and it is the great Staircase here with its first-floor Hall and dome above which is one of the triumphs of Berrington. A great, coffered arch spans one side of the room, with a small arch tucked away within its recesses, giving a sense of shadow, almost of mystery, against the flood of light which draws the eye towards the staircase rising majestically upwards round three sides of the room. The bronzed openwork balustrading is light, yet almost hypnotic to the eye, rather like the Greek key pattern: it compels and elevates the gaze upwards to the domed skylight which rises from the fine, painted and moulded ceiling above the Hall on the upper floor, itself surrounded by simple, cool grey-yellow marble columns. Here, clearly, Holland was allowed to have his way, and in its cool austerity set against rich, calm ornament, he has achieved a masterpiece in the neo-Classical style he loved. The uncluttered proportions allow for the richness of the moulded and gilded cornice and ceiling; and the light tracery of the glass dome, like a spider's web against the morning sky, prevents any chance of that surfeit of opulence which spoils so many rooms and so many designs – as though the artist, or his commissioners, did not know when to stop the work.

The major rooms of the house are in a more elaborate style, but fine examples of what the great architect could achieve in other directions and in other styles when he so desired.

To the right of the Entrance Hall is the Library, a room of noble proportions with fine pedimented finishings flanked by pillasters on the fireplace wall and the two shelved walls. The moulded ceiling has medallions of heads of English authors dating from Chaucer to Addison round a central boss, from which is suspended an octagonal pendant candelabra of elegant, unpretentious design and proportion. Over the marble mantelpiece is a framed frieze which is said to depict Homer receiving tributes from the children of the Muses, who are themselves portrayed in the larger medallions gracing the corners of the room.

Opposite the Library is the Drawing-room, and here the ceiling is exceptional in more senses than one, for it celebrates the wedding of Thomas Harley's daughter to the son of the great Admiral in 1781. Moulded in high relief, it depicts cupids holding seahorses by blue-ribboned reins; and the brightly painted medallions of Jupiter, Cupid and Venus, set in formal borderings with exuberant floral sprays, carry on the motif of joy, and love, and great delight. The room itself is spacious, and the walls have almost severely plain moulded panelling, perhaps to offset the riotous festivity of the ceiling. The mantelpiece has caryatids flanking it, and there are (an unusual touch) Wedgwood cameos set in the steelwork of the grate it encloses.

Opening out of this room is the Boudoir, a room obviously built both to house beauty and to bring to mind Venus and her charms, delightful with its beautiful lapis lazuli columns. The ceiling is white, with pinks and blues and medallions depicting Venus playing with Cupids whilst swans and rosettes alternate around the frieze. The shell-like formation of the curved ceiling above the columns recalls the naval match made by the daughter of this house – or perhaps it is just another reminder of the goddess of love who is said to have arisen from the sea.

Adjoining the Boudoir is the Smoking-room, at the north-west corner of the house, whilst on the east corner is the Dining-room. Here again the ceiling is decorated, and the central medallion represents, very suitably, a banquet of the gods. This is surrounded by plaster swags and sprays, and at the far ends are panels which represent the activities of Ceres and Bacchus. The moulding of the cornice itself is restrained and formal, off-setting the more extravagant painting and gilding of the actual ceiling. Here again the mantelpiece is of marble, lavishly ornamented, and with laurel wreaths on the two top panels of the side-pieces, which also portray rods, or possibly formalised trumpets, wreathed with vines. The naval influence once again is strong, for standing on the top of the one trumpet is a figure of a woman, probably Britannia, with shield and trident beside her; on the other is a male figure carrying a stork, with, beside him, a ship in full-rig and a naval fort. (He seems to be having some difficulty controlling either the stork or his short, flowing robe!)

One room is called, charmingly, the Justice Room, and another the Sportsman's Room, though there are gun-rooms also provided in the usual manner. Behind the house proper spread out the servants' wings, with halls and rooms and bedrooms which would put many of our modern council houses to shame.

Naturally enough, in a book of this length, there must always be houses left out through sheer limitations of space; but equally there are some which could never be left out. Everyone may have different ideas as to which these are, but from a host of names I would pluck out EYE MANOR as an essential ingredient of this particular dish, not because of any elements in its history, but sheerly on account of the very beautiful moulded ceilings it contains. Although a comparatively small house with nothing about it of the palatial status, it clearly was made for living in and for enjoying; and this latter feature is still available to all who see it today.

It was built *c.* 1680 for Ferdinando Gorges – not, as is sometimes supposed, the Fernando Gorges of Elizabeth's court, and founder of Maine, but a Barbados slave-trader who was known, picturesquely and accurately, as the King of the Black Market. Whatever faults there may have been with his ethics, however, these are certainly not reflected in his aesthetic taste. The house itself is not spectacular exteriorly, but pleasant and dignified, being simple brick, of five bays, two-storeyed, with a pitched roof and windows which were altered in the late 18th century. In the basement are the remains of the original stone windowing, with mullions and square heads. For my personal taste the alteration has been all to the good.

But the interior must be seen to be fully appreciated. The staircase is wide, leading to an upper landing which has three-quarter panelling all round it. Three of the walls have elaborate cornice and pediment ornaments, supported by side pilasters and decorated, respectively, with the much-loved escallop and swags of the period, as well as the Gorges and Hilliard coats-of-arms.

The ceiling of the Entrance Hall is divided into nine panels by large, moulded plaster beams, or trabeations, set well below the actual panels, and these have moulded rosettes at the intersections. The panels themselves, offset by the deep frame of the beams, are enriched with swags of drapery, flowers and fruit. It is a truly splendid ceiling to greet the guest, and many feel that it is one of the finest in Herefordshire.

In the south-east room, which is large and rectangular, the ceiling has a beautifully delineated geometric design, combining broken circles and squares and rectangles, as though some giant jigsaw puzzle has been carefully arranged on the ceiling, each piece deliberately separated from its fellow, and so allowing the half-moon shapes to be clearly off-set by the straight lines. The central design is a circle expanded by the addition of shaped panels to enhance the opposition of curve and straight line so intriguingly planned, and the whole centres on a simple circle, or wreath, in the middle of the intricacies thus achieved. Wreaths of exotic fruits, flowers and foliage riot across the panels, scrolled acanthus luxuriate along the four rectangular panels, and figures sport amongst the sprays with a gay abandon in their gestures which perfectly matches the exuberance of this whole magnificent ceiling. The other rooms have similarly elaborate mouldings, one with the coats-of-arms of Gorges and his wife, and their crests, set beside a restrained and dainty circlet of roses, daisies and other simple garden flowers, as though betokening a lovers' posy. Tradition has it that Gorges brought over Italian plasterers to work on his ceilings. Certainly whoever made and designed them were craftsmen and artists of the highest calibre.

High amongst the thick woods of Dinmore Hill lies DINMORE MANOR, the house which still has a tiny chapel of the Knights Hospitallers facing it across its lawn. Originally the chapel and the commandery attached to it were built on the route of the old Roman road which crossed over into Wales, and the settlement was dedicated to St John the Evangelist, the patron saint of travellers. The monkish settlement began sometime before 1190, when it became linked up with the Knights Hospitallers and the dedication was transferred to St John of Jerusalem. Its importance may be gauged by the fact that the Commandery of of Dinmore ranked third amongst the fifty-odd commanderies in England and Wales. When the Order was dissolved in 1540, the Dinmore estates passed through the Wolrych family until the early 18th century, when they passed to the Flemings, then to the St Johns. In 1927 it was bought by the Murray family, the present owners.

There is little left of the twelfth-century chapel, which was for the most part rebuilt in the 14th century; but it still stands there, a small, grey stone building on smooth, green lawns, looking across at the modern manor-house that has been built on the site of the sixteenth-century building erected when the Hospitallers' commandery came into lay hands. Until the end of the 18th century a circular, stone pigeon-house existed, but this has gone now, one of the last links with a particular way of life lived in these old, semi-monastic commanderies.

The south side of the house which was built in the 19th century as an addition to the older sixteenth-century part, contains stones from the still older fourteenth-century buildings, and it includes two sixteenth-century fireplaces as well as a later Jacobean one, together with a considerable amount of panelling of the same era. The large Music Room and the Cloisters have been added on by Richard Hollins Murray, and lie to the east of the older house. The Music Room is in the style of a baronial hall, and is 67ft by 25ft, and 34ft high. The mullioned windows have coloured glass scenes of knights in the times of the Crusades. At one end is a bay with a great stone fireplace in it and a low arch which cuts it off slightly from the vastness of the rest of the hall. Above it is a small room with a three-light window projecting into the Music Room, and above this again is a gilded bronze statue of St George standing in a niche in the wall.

Beyond the Music Room lie the Cloisters, which run along two sides of the lawn and face out towards the old chapel at the far end of the garden. At the south end is an octagonal room, appropriately enough called the South Room, from which a circular stone stairway allows access to the Cloister-roof, giving fine views of the surrounding hills. Partly built into the room is a small round tower with lancet windows enriched with coloured glass, one of which depicts St John of Jerusalem. At the junction of the two cloister walks is the Grotto Room, where the effect of a grotto and two pools of water is further enhanced by the muted lighting coming from a coloured glass window which throws greeny-blue shadows over all. From the Grotto the water passes under the Cloisters and out into the pools of the Rock Garden, which lies just outside the southern Cloister. The stream, dropping from pool to pool on its different levels, is spanned by a small stone bridge, but always the eye is drawn towards that small building on the far side which seems to dominate even the beautiful water-plants and the many-hued shrubbery of this quiet spot – the little chapel built for the Knights of God, who served him by offering hospitality, shelter and nursing care to the traveller on the old Roman road.

Perhaps it is not inappropriate that Dinmore Manor, of Knights Hospitallers fame, was the home the late Charles Ian Murray who served modern travellers so well as regards safe motoring. For Mr Murray was the inventor of the cat's eyes which are such a boon to motorists along dark roads. Although, for various reasons, he personally did not patent the invention or benefit from it, he had the consolation of knowing that his invention must have saved thousands of lives; and also that Dinmore Manor is the only house in England which is allowed to have a sign, which may be seen on the main Hereford-Leominster road, with the name worked out in cat's eyes.

Some distance away, set in the woods of a little valley and reached by a road which is little more than a track, lies LOWER BROCKHAMPTON, the sort of gem which is the more enhanced for the natural beauty of its surroundings still safely enclosing it. Here is a moated manor-house of the 14th century just as it must have looked all those centuries ago, with a detached timber-framed Gatehouse of the 15th century. Nearby are the ruins of the twelfth-century chapel which once existed, so people must have lived here even before the lovely old house was built. The timbering shows different styles and different ages, all grown together into one beautifully integrated whole. The medieval Hall inside has beams and a cruck truss and collar beams which must have delighted the hearts of those who built them 600 years or so ago. The floors are dark with age, and the latticed windows sparkle gaily as though glad that people still come to admire them and remark on their beauty. Sitting in its wooded throne the old house seems to preen itself as a young girl might do, and perhaps with more reason – for it has retained its beauty through so many years and grown lovelier with passing time. I think it must be well pleased with its reflection in the encircling moat.

CROFT CASTLE was held by the Croft family since before 1066 and up to 1745 – a long time by any reckoning. Then Sir Archer Croft, the third Baronet, sold the property and it passed through several hands until in 1923 the Trustees of the late Sir James Croft, Bt, bought it back, since when it has again remained in the hands of the family. The present owner, Lord Croft, bought back the remainder of the estate also, and finally arranged for the transfer of the whole to the National Trust, at the same time finding the very large endowment needed by the National Trust if it were to preserve the building properly and suitably for the nation.

It stands some way off the road, but may be seen to great advantage from it, set amongst its trees and parkland, a tiny chapel standing beside with its odd cupola bell-turret seeming so strangely out of place next to the old fortified mansion, yet at the same time very much at home.

Croft Castle is built in typical quadrangular style, with circular towers at the corners, and dates from the 14th and 15th centuries. According to Robinson there was no wall between the two eastern towers in the middle of the 18th century, access then being gained through the open courtyard and via a doorway in the western wing. This was probably done during the Elizabethan era, when it was perhaps felt that there was no longer any need for it to retain its fortifications, it being made into a mansion rather than a *domus defensabilis*. It may have been this which made the Royalists decide not to use it as a garrison so that the Roundheads also would make no attempt to use it.

Somewhere between 1750-60 the east side was renewed, having projecting bays *à la Gothique* built on. Under the hands of Richard Knight, who owned it during the late 1700s, a good deal of Gothic decoration was undertaken; and the Gothic style is much in evidence today. It is an interesting example of the way in which Gothic can be used in old buildings, and since it is open to the public at certain times under the National Trust it is a house which no visitor to the area should miss.

It may be debatable whether or not we can call a school a house, or a home, even when inhabited by boarder-pupils; but, architecturally, LUCTON SCHOOL just cannot be passed over without comment, and since it is so near Croft Castle it will certainly be seen by those going to the latter.

Lucton was built in 1708 by John Pierrepont, a member of the great philanthropic family of the later Pierrepont-Morgans – the founding member, perhaps. Both his philanthropy and his taste seem to have been uncommonly well developed, and Lucton is a fine example of the best type of school building of its era – an era when the importance of a full, classical and scientific education was becoming more and more widely recognised.

Pleasant lawns and well-trimmed trees stand in front of the old original building, which faces on to the road. It is seven-bayed, with a deep, comfortable-looking hipped roof – not one of those which look likely to slide off at any moment. This roof is in good proportion to the rest of the building and looks as though it were built to last. The edifice is of red-brick, and the three central bays project under a pediment in which is set a clockface with the Piers crest and initials in a scroll-work surround, and with the date 1708. Below, in a deep, arched niche, stands a nearly life-sized figure of the founder, a statue which gives him such an air of liveliness and interest, even in wood, that the original must have been a most intriguing personality indeed. In the Dining-room is a beautiful marble cartouche, carved by a Flemish craftsman, one Jan van Ost, and commemorating the life and work of the founder. On the chimney-stack, on the east wall of the house, is a small panel which reads: 'Ex sumptibus Johannis Pierrepont'; and one hopes that the boys who pass it daily really do appreciate that this place was given out of a good man's goodness of heart and bounty, and not, as the much-vaunted comprehensive schools, out of taxes culled from over-burdened taxpayers, rich and poor alike, without distinction. It must have been the generosity of his nature, as much as of his funds, which has made Lucton School such a fine memorial to John Pierrepont's memory.

26. Bosbury House. A Georgian house of considerable charm and dignity with additions of 1873

27. The Old School House at Marden. with its thatched roof, an unusual feature in Herefordshire

28. **Whitbourne Hall**, a dignified Classical mansion drawn up as late as 1860 by Edward Evans, with a fine colonnaded entrance portico
29. **Dinmore Manor**, showing the fourteenth-century chapel, the modern cloisters and the nineteenth-century south face of the old manor house

30. Berrington Hall. A masterpiece of Henry Holland's work, the dome and painted ceiling over the Staircase is one of the triumphs of Berrington

31. Berrington Hall. The magnificent Staircase with delicate balustrading

32. Berrington Hall, shell-like formation of Boudoir's curved arch ceiling

33. Croft Castle. The central portion of the east face was added in 1750-60 between the two original fourteenth-century towers

34. Croft Castle. The Blue Room, with its beautiful moulded ceiling and medallion-panelled walls displays a fine Gainsborough over the fire-place

Chapter 6

BY ARROW, BY LUGG

WEOBLEY, which is an artist's paradise, is so full of fascinating houses of all manner of dates that a whole book could be written on it alone. Most good guide-books refer to the various houses which throng the centre of the town, and there is a local publication giving very full and interesting details. Collectors of old cruck truss buildings find all their wildest dreams fulfilled as they hunt around the area. Because of this it would be superfluous to write much about Weobley here.

THE OLD VICARAGE, however, deserves a mention as it is often missed, lying as it does on the road leading out of the town. This is a very delightful building, black-and-white timber-framed, with upper bowed windows supported by carved finials. From one of the door jambs of the front door a man's face carved in dark old wood smiles out at all who pass. And, at the other end of Weobley, by The Unicorn, is a house called THE THRONE, reputed to have sheltered King Charles during his wanderings here. The Unicorn claims the honour of having fed him, so I suspect the meals were cooked there and he slept at The Throne, strange though the whole arrangement may seem. The house is long and low, two-storeyed, with timber-framing and a medley of variously styled windows. It is said to have been built in the late 16th or early 17th century, on an *L*-shaped plan. The west gable of the east wing has fine, enriched barge-boards, and inside there are exposed beams on the ceilings which doubtless looked down with pity on the unhappy monarch in his perplexities.

At Luntley, turning sharply into the village by a narrow lane, stands LUNTLEY COURT, on the right hand side of the road, with its charming Dovecote in a field on the other side of the road. The old Court is a long, timber-framed house with a porch which would seem to have been added somewhat later, and is unusual in that it is entered from the sides, with charming wooden balusters across the front of the porch and the date 1674 carved in it. The Dovecote might come straight out of some fairy-tale, with its lovely little four-gabled stone roof and timber-framed sides.

Coming down from the hill from Luntley into Pembridge, a building standing on raised ground catches the eye just before the old Market Hall and New Inn are reached. It is the admixture of building styles and eras which calls for attention, since each side seems different. Then, delight or delights, passing the end of the drive the old timbered outbuildings come into view. The foremost of these, visible from the road, has a gabled cross-wing with a central arch, through which once the big wains would have passed piled high with hay. The head beam of the archway rests on two shaped wooden brackets, and there is a small window set in the timbering above, as there is also in the two end gables of the old barn. Behind is another range of timbered outbuildings, and once there was a third, similar range, which has now unfortunately been pulled down.

There must have been some sort of homestead here for very many centuries, long before it was a farm. There is evidence of a mound, of the sort on which the first fortified wooden castles were built; and of a moat, east of the present house, roughly square, though now partly filled in on the west side. Even the name has very ancient connotations. It is believed that before the 17th and 18th centuries COURT HOUSE had been owned by the Bengoughs, who eventually bought it back for some years during the 19th century, before selling it once more. The lordship of the borough of Pembridge appears to have been entirely separate from that of the Manor, and was held for long by the Coningsbys of Hampton Court, being eventually sold by the Earl of Essex in about the 18th century. It may have been because of his friendship with the then Earl of Essex that Dr William Sherborne purchased the house upon his preferment to the Rectory of Pembridge. Robinson advises us that he was 'a well-beneficed divine of some eminence, an intimate friend of the Earl of Essex, and a sufferer for loyalty to his sovereign.'

Court House is recorded in the *R.C.H.M.* as being of two storeys, with cellars, built on a rectangular plan in the early 17th century but much altered in the 18th century.

Inside the rooms are well proportioned, and the middle room on the north side is lined with Queen Anne panelling, whilst there are several doors of the same date in various rooms. Two of the rooms on the west side are also lined with eighteenth-century panelling, with dado rail and cornice, and the fireplaces have moulded surrounds. Several rooms, including the Kitchen, have exposed ceiling beams, and in the latter the great bacon hooks are still in place. There is an old bread-oven in the Storeroom, whilst the cool Dairy has its slabs and trough still intact.

Court House is mentioned in MacDonald's and Sinclair's *History of Herefordshire Cattle*, where there is a picture of the house as it was in 1909, together with the information that 'Mr Edward Price, of Court House, Pembridge, bred and owned some of the most distinguished animals of the Herefordshire breed', he having, in 1849, 'won the first prize at the Norwich Meeting of the Royal Agricultural Society of England with Sir David 349.' It is apparently an established fact that there are few herds of Herefords of any note in the county in which the blood of the Court House Herd is not to be found. It therefore makes the proud claim of being one of the original homes of the famous Herefordshire breed of cattle.

The orginal stone chimneys, which would appear to have been Jacobean in style, have been replaced by dark-coloured brick ones, perhaps losing a little of the warmth which mellowed red-brick might have given, but certainly adding to the sense of character of the whole house.

Eardisland is one of those strange little places which one seems to stumble on before being really prepared for it; a few houses, the village shop and post office, and then, round a bend, suddenly a cluster of black-and-white houses, two inns, appropriately enough called The White Swan and The Cross, and an old stone bridge. On the calm surface of the river which flows under it swans do their graceful, easy gliding, and ducks criss-cross in fussier, more confusing lines; yet all seem to live together peacefully enough under the trailing branches of the willow trees which fan the surface of the waters here.

Over the bridge is the place I had come to see, the memory of which I had carried so long and happily in my mind – the OLD STAICK HOUSE, originally the Mote House, or council chamber, the place where justice was dispensed; call it what you will, a lovely building more akin perhaps to a manorial home than anything else in the village.

But disappointment awaited me.

The graceful outlines of the house, built and added to from the 14th to the 17th centuries, were still there, but it was like a ghost of its former self. The peacocks cut out of the centuries old yews that form the hedge and entrance archway, had vanished – a slightly unsightly jagged upward-turned bough all that remained of one of the tails. The old latticed windows no longer gleamed and winked in the sunlight, but were dull, like old, faded eyes peering out across the garden. The tiny bay formed by a two-paned latticed window still projected above the first storey under one eave, and I had always longed to know what sort of room lies behind it. But I was fated not to find out that day; and I only hope that by the time I can visit it once more the beautiful old house may be restored to its original loveliness again with its dark timbers framing crisp white plaster, and the sheltering arms of the three front portions of the old building enclosing again a trim lawn and fragrant shrubs. Once there was reputed to be a chapel-room in the roof amongst the immense old trefoil and quatrefoil timbers, but whether it is there now I was unable to find out. Once, also, a wide oak staircase with fine newels and bannisters. I suspect it remains, along with the great open fireplaces which have watched centuries pass by.

Some sites are an open invitation to any man with a building urge. In sterner times than ours they were places usually endowed with military advantages, clearly designed by Nature as observation posts, or with geo-physical features which made them admirable situations for fortified outposts. Fortified look-outs were not a convenience but a necessity in this Border country. Later, less-troublous centuries recognised in them the ideal beauty spot for gracious homes and gracious living, blessed with panoramic views, with wooded hills to delight the eye and content the soul, and with fertile acres to ensure good agricultural rewards.

BURTON COURT, near Eardisland, stands in just such a place, a high spot which was an ancient British camp long before the Romans came to these parts. Tradition points out a mound standing a little west of the house, surmounted by a great Blue Atlas cedar tree, which has always been known as The Camp. So far no systematic archaeological excavations have been attempted, so that it cannot be said for certain whether it was ever occupied during Roman times, nor whether it was ever used again during the Dark Ages, as were so many of the old encampments.

It is certain, however, that the Manor of Burton featured in *Domesday*, so it is likely that a building had existed here for some little time before that. After that date, however, there is a gap of some 250 years until the surviving *Rolls* of the Manor take up the tale in 1331, in the reign of Edward III. The first Lord of the Manor given in the *Rolls* at that time is Thomas St Owen. In 1402, Henry, Prince of Wales, later to become Henry V, made the spot his headquarters during his campaign against the Welsh rebel, Owen Glyndwr. It was an excellent viewpoint from which to survey the movements of the enemy coming down from the far Welsh hills and laying waste the surrounding countryside. It was within easy communication of outlying posts and scouting parties. The only part of the present building which Henry of Agincourt would have known is the old fourteenth-century Great Hall, the beautiful timbered roof of which was exposed about 1865 when the then ceiling was removed; a most happy decision which, probably unwittingly, brought this great treasure to light. The *R.C.H.M.* gives a good description of this fine medieval roof: '. . . early 14th century, of five bays, with curved braces below collar beams, forming two centred arches; the upper edges of the collar beams are cusped, and there are two ranges of cusped windbraces below the purlins.'

In the early 18th century the house was apparently a long, low, half-timbered structure incorporating the Great Hall, probably as its central portion, which is the usual pattern, and gradually added to in later centuries on either side. Up to that time it had had several owners since the days of the St Owen family mentioned in the *Rolls*. One of the daughters married into the Tyrells of Brinsop Court, and eventually, by marriage, the house came into the possession of the Downtons. From them it passed to John Cotes, of Cotes in Staffordshire and Woodcote in Shropshire, and continued in that family until the reign of Charles I. For a short while after that it passed to one of the branches of the Crofts of Croft Castle, but it was sometime before 1700 when it came into the possession of the Brewsters, the family with whom it is perhaps most closely associated, and who retained it until 1865, when the last Brewster heiress and her husband, the Revd Canon W. E. Evans, died without heir. In 1865 it was bought by John Clowes, and it continued in the Clowes family until the estate was broken up in 1949.

A large house such as Burton Court was not always an asset in the 1950s, with the steadily increasing decay of agricultural life and the difficulties of staffing. Finally it was sold again, and bought by the present owner, Lt-Cdr R. M. Simpson, whose imaginative treatment of the house and its potential has made it again a centre of life and activity which would delight its past owners. For apart from the business side of growing soft fruit, Lt-Cdr Simpson and his wife have gathered together here an Exhibition of Costumes and Curios which is open to the public during the summer months and is proving a great attraction.

The approach is by a drive which sweeps upward to a broad forecourt in front of the house. Apart from the Great Hall, now disguised externally so that it merges with the rest of the more recent additions, most of this frontage is Regency, but additions were made to the house in the 1860s by Kempson; and in 1912 Sir Clough Williams-Ellis, designer of Portmeirion and other items of great architectural interest, was brought in to design the present entrance, with its semi-circular flight of steps leading up to the deep porch. This replaced the older entrance leading directly into the Great Hall, which had a Gothic-type porch to match the then Gothic-type windows of the Hall. Tall, graceful mullioned windows flank the entrance now; but at the far end the curved glass windows, often a feature of interest in Regency design, describe a broad bay, originally to form the Dining-room of the house but now used for exhibition purposes. The present Dining-room is on the far side, a finely-proportioned room with a moulded and gilded ceiling of formal geometrical design, and tall, floor-length windows in the bay looking out on to the terrace and gardens beyond. The curtains, of a dark grey-green pattern, with a hint of bronze which fits beautifully into the cool, dignified décor of the room, were brought from nearby Hampton

Court when the Earl of Hereford's estate there was sold up. The furniture, designed in 1882 for a house in Sutton Coldfield, was intended to ensemble with a remarkable mantelpiece there depicting Shakespearian characters in bronze, and makes for a most interesting feature in this room. On one wall is a small oil painting of Queen Elizabeth I, by Zucchero, the court painter of the period; and the eyes-and-ears pattern on the rich orange-brown material of her costume is a symbolic reminder of the reality of her almost omniscient power and insight in matters relating to her kingdom.

In the Entrance Hall, stretching along almost the entire length of one wall, is a modern, machine-worked tapestry, whose muted browns blend in perfectly with the warm gleams of the polished wood furniture. An especial feature is the lovely semi-circular flying staircase with its graceful sweep and open balustrading. Each tread is composed of one tapering block of stone cantilevered into the main wall, lending an effect of great up-soaring lightness, which has given the name of 'flying' to this type of unsupported stairway.

The panels between the Dining-room and Library are of particular interest in that they were carved by the late Mrs Clowes, one of whose hobbies was woodcarving. Their simple, formal Tudor-rose design achieves a pleasant sense of repose which more elaborate forms might have missed. A beautiful water-colour of the many-gabled old Hereford Town Hall, with its fine timbered panels and latticed windows, by Paul Braddon, hangs on one wall of the Library and reminds viewers of the house's links with Hereford, for the well-known Dr William Brewster had his town-house, the old Mansion House, in Hereford. A scholar of some considerable eminence, the county as a whole has benefitted by his generosity, though the house itself may have lost inestimable treasures, since when he died in 1715 he left his magnificent collection of books to All Saints Church, Hereford, where they have formed one of Hereford's two famous chained libraries. This factor in itself is a rarity, as this was a complete library, a one-off as it were, instead of a gradual accumulation of volumes by various donors, as is more usual.

It is mainly in the Great Hall that the collection of Costumes and Embroideries is housed when on display, and it is a magnificent setting for such a period collection. The great five-panelled carved overmantel is Cromwellian, and dated 1654. The *R.C.H.M.* description reads: 'The fireplace in the West wall has an overmantel made up of two ranges of enriched arcaded panelling with terminal figures; flanking the fireplace are two terminal figures of angels of foreign origin.' It is well worth study in itself, if time can be spared from the other items of interest around the room.

After some considerable searching, the Simpsons managed to locate the original oil portraits of the Brewster family stacked away in the storerooms of the Hereford City Museum, to which they had been bequeathed by a member of that family. Dusty, and a little more than musty, with the frames long since removed and untraceable, a request was nevertheless made that they should be loaned back to Burton Court. The reply, that if the Simpsons were prepared to bear the cost of reframing them they could have them on loan may seem slightly lacking in that sense of propriety and civic responsibility in which the donors of such gifts have such simple faith. However, it is hoped that in the future these portraits will once more hang on the walls of the staircase, looking down approvingly, I have no doubt, on the activities wthin their old ancestral home.

No visitor to Herefordshire should miss this lovely old house with its wonderful display of family costumes worn through the centuries, and Lt-Cdr and Mrs Simpson are to be congratulated in having opened their home to the public for a project which is not only of considerable educational value, but also gives so much aesthetic pleasure to visitors.

Tucked away among the hills that line the A480 lies BRINSOP COURT. This is of particular interest in that from whichever side it is approached it gives an entirely different aspect, more than six centuries having gone into its building. Extensive renovations and alterations have now been carried out in a way which has combined imaginative use of modern ideas and techniques with a deep appreciation of the charm and character of the whole.

Approaching it from the A480, the first glimpse of it comes just before the lane takes a sharp left-handed turn. Across the fields the slightly gaunt walls of a typical fourteenth-century baronial hall can be seen with, adjoining it, a slightly more modern building, probably nearer the 15th century than the original part, its mullioned windows less severe than the narrower ogee-headed ones of its parent building. As the lane veers off and straightens out again the Georgian west side of the building comes into view, dreaming above a wide, rippling moat, just the sort of moat Mariana in *Mariana in the Moated Grange* must have looked out onto in her weary wait. One might wonder why it was Tennyson who wrote the poem, and not Wordsworth, who had associations with Brinsop and stayed here on several occasions.

A sharp, right handed turn brings one to tall gate-piers, the lane continuing through them and then, within a very few yards, branching off left on to the road at the top of the slight incline or, right, into the private grounds of Brinsop Court. Here again are tall gate-piers, surmounted by figures of horses attacked by leopards, lovely groups weathered to deep metallic greens which are offset by the stone of the pier-columns.

From the lane the lovely north front of the building may be seen fully, with the moat and two ponds separated by narrow causeways and surrounded by shrubs and weeping willows sighing and moving restlessly as the wind ripples across the wide expanse of water. It is a beautiful setting, and one feels – or should feel! – a sense of gratitude that the owners of such a home have not hidden it from view behind high hedges or walls, but left it open to the gaze of passers-by that they may share its loveliness.

Robinson tells us that according to an old manuscript the Court 'was originally moated around, and approached by a drawbridge. Within the quadrangle was a chapel with a crypt beneath it, a dungeon, and a blacksmith's forge. The chapel with the staircase leading to it, occupied one side of the square; it had a groined roof and walls painted in frescoes . . . two towers flanked the drawbridge, having grotesque figures on their tops, one being a monkey playing with a fiddle. In the inner court was a third tower which, though in a perfect state of preservation, was pulled down about fifty years ago to assist in building a wall round the stables.'

On the whole, this sounds more like the work of a vivid imagination, or a misunderstanding of the original purposes of the building, than an accurate account, since what is there called the chapel, with crypt and dungeon beneath it, is quite evidently an excellent example of a typical baronial hall. It is uncertain whether two towers would in fact have flanked the drawbridge, and there appears to be little architectural evidence to support this; but there are indications of a turret, or small tower, in the courtyard, since doorways in the corner of the rooms below it still remain. It is interesting to note, in old drawings of Brinsop, that the staircase to the Hall has been moved to the far end rather than being in the middle of the range. It would be interesting to know which had been the original position.

The first Lord of Brinsop actually recorded as such was Ralph Torell, or Tirell, in 1210. Sometime before the 15th century it seems to have come into the hands of the Daunteseys or Danseys, in whose possession it remained until the late 18th century. The poets Wordsworth and Southey often visited Brinsop, as the then tenant, a Mr Hutchinson, was Wordsworth's brother-in-law. It is said that the poet wrote several poems whilst here, the best known being that on the legend of St Katherine of Ledbury. There are windows to Wordsworth, his wife, sister and daughter in Brinsop church, a short way off across the fields, and he is believed to have planted a cedar tree on the lawn, though I understand that this was blown down in 1915.

Lovers of *Kilvert's Diary* may also recall that the young Vicar of Bredwardine recorded a visit to Brinsop in his Diary – the last entry, indeed, and dated 13 March 1879: 'Lunch at Brinsop Vicarage . . . In the afternoon I walked with Mr. Fowle to the church and then across the meadows to Brinsop Court. We met a fine old lady waiting with a staff as high as her shoulder. A young woman in a scarlet cloak was with her. A fine sunset gleam lit up the grand old manor-house and the lawn and the two snow-white swans on the flowing water of the moat. On the lawn grew the cedar planted by William wordsworth the poet. Young Mr. Edwards (the tenant of the farm, which belongs to the Ricardo family) was carpentering in the greenhouse. He courteously took us into a noble sitting-room Turkey carpeted and nicely furnished with a fine painting of the poet over the chimney piece. And here dear Dorothy Wordsworth spent much of her time.'

In view of the prestige in which old buildings are held today and the endeavours made by men high and low to preserve what remains to us of our heritage, it comes as a shock to realise how little concern was often shown in the past for what we regard as great architectural treasures; for at the beginning of the last century the Great Hall was being used as a granary, its former dignity and aesthetic merits being totally disregarded.

The north side of the building is two-storeyed, warm red-sandstone, mostly of the 14th century, with a massive arched double door, heavily studded, and obviously made to keep out more than just the wind. The windows along this range are mainly small two-light windows, though at one end is a larger transomed window. The building at the eastern end is sixteenth-century timber-framed.

The short drive leads into a paved courtyard. Once the moat flowed past here, but it has now been piped underground on this side of the building and certainly makes for easier access.

But the real surprise lies in store when one steps inside the great double door to a small, fairly narrow hallway with old wooden walling and another old, single, studded door immediately facing the main doorway. When this is opened it opens into the Hall proper – a square room under the timbered gateway overhead, with doors leading off left and right, but full-length glass sliding doors looking out into the old original courtyard of the house. These have replaced the windows which used to be here, and the alteration is a really excellent and imaginative piece of planning; for the sense of coming through the old gateway and directly into the courtyard as the original occupants must have done is very strong. Only the lack of blustery wind acts as a reminder that there is in fact a glass screen separating the Hall from the courtyard, as effectively as the centuries separate it from the knights-at-arms who rode through and dismounted by the steps of the Great Hall on the far side.

Today the stone-flagged courtyard has roses growing in it, probably lovelier than any its old occupants ever knew; and from inside the house it is even easier to appreciate the different stages of growth which this building has undergone. On the far side, and at the far end of the courtyard stands the Great Hall, an excellent example of its period and typical in every respect. A flight of stone steps leads up to the iron-studded door in the ogee-headed archway on the first floor, where the lord and family and their retainers would have lived. The windows on the ground floor, which would have been mainly for storage, are smaller, single-light ones; but the rest of the building on this side was obviously added some years later, and its ground-floor windows are mullioned and are, in fact, the windows of the present Dining-room. All along the eastern end of the courtyard, and adjoining the Great Hall, is a range of pink-washed timbered buildings, mostly added during this century but entirely in keeping with the earlier portions of timbering of the 16th century and the early-seventeenth-century work on the older north range of buildings. Set beside the stern stone-work of the Great Hall they present a most charming foil of grace and relaxation. Part of the timbering continues, merging in with the older stone portions along the north range, and leading up to the gateway which, on this interior side, has a timbered frontage to the gabled room above the old arch. Eventually the pleasant admixture of timbering and original stonework on this side merges into the brickwork of the western end of the courtyard, where the Georgian building adds its own peculiar grace to the whole.

Inside, the house is as full of surprises as its exterior. The room on the left of the entrance-arch still has its old ceiling beams, with stone walls and timbered walls, and with two-light windows of the 14th century watching outwards towards the world, and later ones viewing the inner courtyard with a less wary aspect. In the corridor on the right of the entrance a broad wooden staircase leads upstairs, and facing it is a large panelled room with windows on either side, looking into the courtyard and out across the moat. There are exposed beams and a huge, open, stone fireplace. An interesting and unusual feature is the wooden open-work screen which divides off the immediate entrance into the room from the rest of it, much as many of the old solars were divided off into a separate portion in the manorial halls. Beyond it, in the far corner of the building, surrounded by the moat on the west and south sides, is a smaller Drawing-room with cream eighteenth-century panelling and the lighter, airier windows of the Georgian period.

The Great Hall still retains the massive timbers of its original open roof; its king-pins and slightly arched tie-beams, with unusual trefoil-shaped struts on each of the four sides of the king-pins, make for special interest in the ceiling work. Three stone, arched windows look out across the meadowland outside, whilst two look down into the central courtyard, and there is a big, stone, open fire with shouldered lintel on the far side of the room. An oil painting of Wordsworth (the one mentioned by Kilvert) hangs now above the door in the Great Hall.

The fifteenth-century part of this range is over the Dining-room below, and now houses the Library. It has two high, mullioned four-light windows in the south wall, between which is a big, open fireplace surmounted by a three-panelled, carved wooden overmantel believed to be Jacobean, with male and female figures. A broad, eight-lighted mullioned window looks across the courtyard to the gateway. How often must the ladies of the house have stood here watching their lord and his knights ride in under that archway, gay and laughing as they returned from a good day's hunting, or droop-weary, swaying in their saddles after some bloodier affray against the invaders who so often swept down from the line of the far Welsh hills! The ceiling in this room is an unusual form of moulded decoration, an odd piece of twentieth-century work of intermediate style, having interlacing patterns and formal sprays in a rather stiff, slightly unimaginative design; but lifted into lighter vein by four circular panels which have a bird, a squirrel, a swan, and another bird in them. The whole ceiling is studded with deep, slightly heavy, pendant bosses, which again are surprisingly linked with other, completely different, styles of decoration by having four small cupid-like figures on them, one on each side.

It is said that ALDER'S END, or Orlder's End, at Tarrington is so called because the land changes here from the higher Bromyard formation to silt washed down from the hills. In Roman times Alder's End was probably a well-defended posting station for the convoys to Kenchester, which was then being built. Until quite recently there were signs of both palisade and ditch defences, with a good system of water supplies, so it would seem that these were kept in repair for centuries after the Romans left, and were probably used against both Saxons and Danes. On the east side of the house there were, until the beginning of this century, an underground kitchen and baking-oven which were said to be centuries old.

In *Domesday Book* there is mention of the Manor of Taddington, and Alder's End is supposed to have been this, since it is clearly the oldest place in the area, very much older than the later Manor. Equally, there are indications around its grounds which qualify it for such a title – a strip of artificially levelled and raised ground on the south of the garden which is meant to have been used for archery practice and, in later times, as a tilt-yard, when life and the defence of property depended on a man's accuracy and skill in 'getting his man'.

In 1350 the manorial rights at Taddington were transferred to the de Barres, probably when Alder's End became a Cistercian house, since such an order could not hold manorial rights. Evidence of their occupation of the original house may be found in the remains of the five fish-ponds adjacent to the house. The Dovecote and some other half-dozen fish-ponds also indicate a station above that of a simple farm.

At the beginning of this century there were apparently still bolts, used to release the water to clean out the pools and irrigate the surrounding meadows, which were scarred with the water-furrows used for irrigation.

In 1551 Henry VIII turned the Cistercians out of Alder's End, as well as out of Little Tarrington which it is believed also belonged to the Brotherhood. Other names remain in the area which seem to support the tradition of a monastery and its lands here once – for instance, The Vine, a name which is often found where once monks ran vineyards efficiently and had a steward living near the site. We tend to forget the terrible collapse of country life resulting from Henry VIII's greed and the Dissolution of the Monasteries. The monasteries usually employed much labour, agricultural, horticultural, and of other forms, often running mills, potteries, pin-making factories and employing many people in various cottage industries. They knew their business and, for their own benefit as much as anything else, ran their estates efficiently and well, so that when a monastery collapsed the economic system and welfare of the surrounding area also suffered a severe decline.

Anyway, under Henry's clenched fist the poor Cistercians left their monastic farm, its quiet pools and vineyards; and with their going passed a way of life which left the countryside for many a year in a state of sheer chaos and unnecessary waste.

From an old painting we know that the pigeon-house was a circular one with a lantern top and, I suspect, was fairly newly-built at the time of the Suppression of the Monasteries. It was, however, fairly modest as pigeon houses go, being merely 16ft in diameter, and it had 576 nesting places. It was cracked by a land tremor in 1896, and collapsed completely when a bomb fell and exploded in Pigeon House Orchard in September 1941. Today the old farmhouse still stands there, cloaking the acres of the past under its newer walls and additions, and the names of the fields all round the area still delight the tongue and the imagination: Plex, Round Batch, Gorsty Piece, Dunsills, Tinker's Orchard, Pigeon House Orchard, Young Orchard, Briar's Farlands, Summerpool, Winter Hill, Oaky Piece – words rubbed a thousand times by use and polished to a homespun roundness and delight by the soft Herefordshire burr of nearly a thousand years.

Beyond Hereford, the bridge at Mordiford – looking towards the church and the old red Vicarage above the River Lugg – is well known to artists and beloved by fishermen. On the hills which rise above it and make such a picturesque background to the setting, stands the home of the old family of the de Herefords, whose ancestors are known to have held lands in Herefordshire and other counties from earliest Norman times, and at Mordiford itself from the reign of Henry III. Today, eight centuries after, the family still lives on its ancestral lands; and its present owners, Maj. and Mrs R. J. Hereford, still take their responsibilities and duties as seriously as did their forebears through the centuries – possibly more so, I am inclined to think, from the way of life they have adopted of their own choice.

OLD SUFTON, the older, earlier home of the Herefords, and at one time a fortified manor house, lies about half a mile away tucked into a rocky hill, in what must have been an excellent strategic position for the needs of the times. Behind it, and on either side, the great hill rises steeply, its rocky scarps, from which the stone for the house was quarried, providing not only a natural defence but also an excellent means of escape when resistance was impossible. Before it, the view commands the whole of the plain surrounding Hereford and away to the Black Mountains and the Welsh Hills, those hills which always posed such a threat to the peaceful life of the countryside, since they housed so many enemies.

At least twice, and possibly three times, in its long history, Old Sufton has been damaged by fire. It is known that a building existed here in 1200, and possibly much earlier; and also that at the time of Richard II, some 200 years later, it was in so dilapidated a condition that the then head of the family, Nicholas de Hereford, tried to evade paying dowry dues to his predecessor's widow, so that he might have more funds for repairing his manor. In Tudor times it was damaged again by fire. Today, having been untenanted for some years prior to renovations and rebuilding being commenced, it has been made sadly derelict by the attentions of young vandals, and now retains fewer and fewer of the earlier points of architectural interest which were incorporated in the sixteenth-century house. These included a chimney stack in the north-west wing which had a thirteenth-century coffin lid built into it with an incised cross on it. There were also mural decorations in a rusty-red, blue, white and grey geometric design, dating from about 1340-50, which were discovered under the wall plaster a few years ago when some repair work was being undertaken. An authority from the Royal Commissions Board described the beams in Old Sufton as some of the largest and oldest he had seen. There is also a very charming medieval Dovecote with an added lantern, which was faced with brick around 1750 and converted into a delightful gazebo. What other features may still be hidden in and under it we can only guess, but perhaps these may be revealed when renovations are put in hand.

Old Sufton had been in uninterrupted occupation by the Hereford family for over 500 years when Sir James Hereford died in 1786. His heir then decided to build the present family home on the hill some half mile nearer to the village.

For the design and construction of SUFTON he engaged the talents of James Wyatt, who was at that time working on the restoration of Hereford Cathedral, and it is Wyatt whom we have to thank for the present very lovely house. Interiorly it is of particular interest in that it has not suffered any serious alterations or renovations since it was built, so we are enabled to appreciate the personality and influence of Wyatt in an almost entire specimen of his total design.

It is a dignified building of dressed Bath stone, in the Classical tradition of the era, and was built *c.* 1790. There are five bays, with two and a half storeys and a full basement. The frontage has a pediment across the centre bay with a door framed by four Ionic columns and a low pediment. At present this has been almost hidden by a glass porch which detracts from the austere and pleasing dignity of the original design, but it is intended to remove this shortly, when the whole of the original frontage will be seen again. The window directly above the main door has two Ionic columns and side pillasters supporting a rounded arch, and the window-frames themselves rest on conventional stone balustrading.

All the bricks and tiles used in the house's building were made on the estate. Tiles in the Wine-cellar have deer spoors and marks of other animals in the surfacing, due to being laid out to dry prior to firing. They would have been trowelled over, but the marks always returned on firing. All the nails, hinges, and similar items were made on the estate; and there is still a cottage known as The Nailers which had a small forge until recently.

Inside, Sufton is a real gem for all who enjoy the light, classical lines of the period, and contains many interesting features of Wyatt's own especial theories. One of these was that interior decoration should always relate to the purpose for which a particular room was intended, and at Sufton this has been carried out *par excellence*. In the original dining-room of the house, which has been used as the Library, however, since the building of new kitchens *c.* 1800, the mouldings of the freize and overmantel depict ears of corn, fruit, and vines; whereas the present Drawing-room, which was the original music-room, has a delightful frieze of musical instruments, and the central panel of the overmantel has a lyre depicted on it. The doors in this room are also extremely interesting. As with all the doors in the rest of the house, the moulded architraves carry reminders of Classical-style pillasters, and have square pedimented heads carrying out the theme of the decoration in the room. But, whereas elsewhere they are all fine, three-panelled, mahogany double doors with the beautiful, perfect proportions of the Classical style, here in the Drawing-room the panels are of mahogany inlaid with ebony and satinwood; and their especial feature is the raised, almost ripple-like fluted effect of the inlaid borders. This apparently was achieved by a particular method of sanding in a hot oven, with pleasing effect.

The shutters to the long, elegant sash windows here are also unusual, in that their panels have delicately moulded, formal geometric patterning on them, and parts of the window embrasures in this room are apparently of terracotta.

With the exception of the original library (now the Dining-room), the mantelpieces on the ground floor are all of marble with moulded surrounds. But, most cunningly disguised, the original library mantelpiece is of marble with a pine surround covered with plaster mouldings to match the décor of the rest of the room. All the upstairs fireplaces and surrounds are also in the same style, save for one, which is entirely of plain marble. All round the house the wooden floors gleam with the patina of nearly two hundred years of care and attention, thus achieving everywhere an effect of warm contrast against the light coloured walls, and the high, white ceilings with their graceful Classical proportions. Here the dark wood panelling of past centuries, and the lower, beamed ceilings of the older style of buildings have been replaced by that sense of light and ease which inevitably takes us back in thought to the magnificent, easy dignity of ancient Greece and Rome.

Originally the kitchens and all the servants' quarters were situated in the basement, and it is particularly fascinating to note the obvious thought and care which Wyatt expended even on these lowly offices. The whole interlinked system of drainage in every room, and of a well-devised water supply, makes one appreciate that he was a true artist, interested not only in architectural style and interior decoration, but also in the smooth and efficient running of the whole establishment, quite literally from top to bottom, so that no part of life lived in his creations should be marred. Shortly after the bitter lessons of the French Revolution had been assimilated by the more thoughtful amongst English minds, it was decided here at Sufton that it might be wiser for the servants to be brought up out of the bowels of the earth, so to speak, and into the bosom of Mother Nature. Accordingly, a whole range of servants' quarters was built, out of doors, but practically adjacent to the house. Whether this was to ensure that the house might not be burned down about their ears, or the throats of the inhabitants slit one dark night by a rebellious mob in the dungeons of the house, or whether it was merely deemed prudent and right to commence on the improvement of working conditions and so prevent a repetition of the events on the Continent, is not quite clear. Suffice it to say that the domestic outbuildings were extremely well planned and commodious, containing, in the manner of the time, not only the usual kitchens, sculleries, store rooms, pantries, bedrooms, servants' hall, butler's rooms, general offices, and so forth, but also the stabling. Even the entrance from the old cellar kitchens into the main Hall of the house was blocked up, and a new entrance was made into the Dining-room. This is perhaps the only slightly displeasing feature of the room, being rather smaller than the two other doors, lacking their full architravure, and also breaking into the symmetry of the moulded panel on the wall and thus proclaiming, almost apologetically, that it was never in the original planning of the room. The old, beautifully planned system of drainage and water supply still remains in the cellars, adapted to the modern needs of the large, modern clothes-washer, and functioning perfectly throughout even after all these years. But, to fit in with the even more modern needs of today and the lack of staff, what was originally the gun-room has been turned into a modern Kitchen, spacious, bright with gay colours and practical working surfaces carefully situated to make working conditions as sensible and easy as possible. No doubt, Wyatt would have approved of these alterations.

The gardens at Sufton were laid out by Repton, in 1795, and the original *Red Book* in which the then up-and-coming young man set forth his suggestions is still in the family archives. The old, walled garden became too expensive to maintain in recent years, and three sides of its walling have been pulled down; but the one wall remaining makes an exquisite background to the trees and shrubs which ensure that the garden is still a delight to the eyes.

Today, after so many centuries, Sufton continues to care for the land its owners have looked after with pride and forethought. Frequently the whole of the low-lying area here at the confluence of the Wye and the Lugg was totally under water during spring and winter floods, considerable injury being done to houses, persons and livestock in the area. Sufton itself is safe from this type of disaster, lying, as it does, high on the hill above the Lugg; but at their own expense Maj. Hereford and his partner Mr John Dorrell have built up about a mile of embankment to mitigate the dangers of flooding to the estate's low-lying farming area. The River Authority has continued the project to lessen the risk to dwellings and land in the villages of the area.

Sufton also boasts one of the largest modern dairy farms in the country, with some 600 dairy cattle and 400 following stock, and hops are grown on the estate just as they have been for years past. The hop harvest has always been gathered and dried by local people, notably by members of one family who have been on the estate since the time of Henry VII.

Maj. and Mrs Hereford feel deeply about the home their ancestors have maintained through eight centuries, and they ensure that it is frequently available to the public, together with its beauties and historical treasures, so that they may be shared by others. Exhibitions of the beautiful collection of lace and embroideries which Mrs Hereford has carefully preserved are held, and these are a delight to students and lovers of old lace alike, covering, as they do, the period of from 1660 to 1850. The collection of fine water-colours by Captain Edward Hereford, who was a naval officer during the last half of the 19th century, is also frequently on show. Some of these are seascapes, many in the style of Turner, and they are pronounced as exceptional by art critics. There is also an interesting painting of Mordiford Church, by Hearn, which shows the famous Mordiford Dragon still in place on the wall.

Copies of the old *Court Rolls* of the Manor of Sufton and other family documents dating from the 12th century are still retained and give a fascinating picture of the way of life through the different ages, the problems of the Lord, and the problems of the poor, the solutions reached and the decisions taken. Some of the original documents are kept at Sufton as examples for visitors who may be interested to see them, but most of the originals have been lent to the County Archives. The house is also frequently open to parties of students who wish to see what is unique in the area as regards this style of architecture, since it has had so few alterations and is not a show-piece, with all the flat formality such buildings garner, but full of the busy atmosphere of daily living; fuller, indeed, than many might suppose from the order which reigns so calmly around.

For some years Sufton formed the home for a co-educational school founded by Mrs Hereford and her mother, Mrs John Dorrell. This continued until the difficulty of obtaining specially trained staff made it impossible to carry on. However, nothing deterred, the Herefords determined that they would continue, in another way, to share their long heritage of peace and beauty in a project about which they both care deeply. For many years they undertook not only the care of their own two children, but also fostered others whose backgrounds for reasons of loss, death, ill-health, and other problems, had been less fortunate. Over the years many children have known Sufton as home, and often return to stay with their 'family' in the old house on the hill in the Herefordshire countryside. Young people from all five continents have stayed at Sufton to learn our language. These young men and women also return and correspond frequently so that the house has become a centre of youthful international communication.

Here, in an area where so many lovely houses of an older era remain, Sufton is unique in its appeal as a country home of the Classical period of English architecture, being of more reasonable proportions than some of the vast, slightly grandiose structures existing elsewhere in England. It is a house which was built to be lived in, a family home, rather than a palatial mansion built for the prestige of its owners and an ostentatious display of wealth. Herefordshire is fortunate in that nearly all her country houses, lesser and greater, are still lived in. And the fact that houses like Sufton retain this particular aspect of their origins, still lived in as a home yet of actual use to the community, makes for a hope that our political leaders, of whatever inclination, will realise the value of such places as part of our national and educational heritage, and make it possible for them to be maintained by their owners and thus available to the general public on occasion.

The tragic loss to the Soviet Union of its historic treasures and heritage, through the wanton destruction of so many of its cultural links after the Revolution, should be a warning to us; as also their later years of frantic scrabbling around trying, too late, to garner something from the glories they had so wastefully and thoughtlessly squandered. Since hope springs eternal, let us cling to the faith that one day government will realise that England's lovely buildings cannot be maintained if their owners are virtually tortured day by day, with the screw tightened constantly by fresh extortions, strangling taxations and rapacious death duties. Their personal loss, tragic though it is to the individuals concerned, is nothing to the loss which we shall suffer as a nation if we allow our present growth to be cut off from the roots which fed and feed it.

It is both the rights and wrongs of history, its glories and its failures, its beauties and its blemishes, which are instilled into the marrow of our bones. We can keep the vital life blood flowing only by accepting that from which we were sprung *in toto* (psychologically, the *Shadow* as well as the *good self*). If the *Shadow* is allowed to take over, to smash and destroy and obliterate all it resents and despises, then we go forward to annihilation. But if its strength, with all its creative potential, be used not only to build a better future, but to preserve all that is good, beautiful and worth-while from the past, then we as a nation can face the future unafraid.

35. The Throne, in Weobley, where Charles I is reputed to have slept

36. Luntley Court is an excellent example of a typical timber-framed manor house

37. Old Staick House at Eardisland, the original justice chamber of the area, displays styles of four centuries

38. Burton Court, near Eardisland, contains a fourteenth-century great hall which today houses a delightful exhibition of costumes and curios

39. Brinsop Court. The fourteenth-century north face of the old manor house where William Wordsworth so often stayed

40. Brinsop Court. Styles from four centuries are mirrored in the placid waters of the manor's broad moat

41. Sufton. Built *c.* 1790 by James Wyatt, the doorways of the present Library are examples of the perfect proportions of the Classical style

42. Sufton, overlooking the Wye at Mordiford, seen through one of the long vistas for which the landscape-gardener Repton was famous

Appendix 1

HOUSES OPEN TO THE PUBLIC

National Trust Properties

(Fuller information regarding viewing, payment, and other details may be obtained from the National Trust, 42 Queen Anne's Gate, London, SW1H 9AS or its Regional Offices, and also from the City of Hereford Tourist Information Centre, Town Hall, Hereford, HR1 2PJ.)

Berrington Hall. 3 miles N. of Leominster, ¼ mile off A49. *Open:* first week in April to end September, Weds, Sats and Bank Holiday Mons, 1400-1800 hrs, or sunset if earlier. At other times during these months by written arrangement with the Estate Office, Berrington Hall, Leominster.
Croft Castle. 5 miles NW. of Leominster, turn north off B4362. *Open:* first Wed. in April to end September, Weds, Thurs, Sats, Suns and Bank Holiday Mons, 1415-1800 hrs. At other times by written appointment with the Caretaker, Croft Castle, Leominster.
The Cwmmau. 4 miles SW. of Kington, between A4111 and A438, approached by a long, narrow private lane. *Open:* April to end September, Bank Holiday Mons and preceding weekends, 1400-1800 hrs, and at other times by previous written arrangement with the tenant, Mr S. M. Joyce.
Lower Brockhampton. 2 miles E. of Bromyard, just N. of A44. *Open:* all year (except January) Mons, Weds, Fris, and Sats, including Bank Holiday Mons, 1000-1300 hrs and 1400-1800 hrs, Suns, 1000-1300 hrs.

Private Properties Open at Certain Times

(The following private properties are open at certain times by kind permission of their owners. Times of opening are given as a guide but visitors are advised to check these before calling. Please remember that, although open to the public at times, these properties are also private residences and their owners' privacy should be respected.)

Burton Court. 5 miles W. of Leominster, between A44 and A4111. *Open:* Spring Bank Holiday to mid-September, Weds, Thurs, Sats, Suns and Bank Holiday Mons, 1430-1800 hrs. Catering facilities are available for parties by previous arrangement with Mrs R. M. Simpson, Burton Court, Eardisland, Leominster – telephone Pembridge 231.
Dinmore Manor. 6 miles N. of Hereford on A49. *Open:* all the year (except Christmas and Boxing Day), 1400-1800 hrs.
Eastnor Castle. 2 miles E. of Ledbury on A438. *Open:* Suns and Bank Holiday

Mons, from end May to end September, 1415-1800 hrs.
Eye Manor. 4 miles N. of Leominster, 1¼ miles W. of A49. *Open:* 28 March to 30 June, Suns, Weds, Thurs and Sats, 1430-1730 hrs. 1 July to 30 September, every afternoon, 1430-1730 hrs. Also Easter and Spring Bank Holiday Mons and following Tues, 1430-1730 hrs.
Hellens. Entrance opposite Much Marcle Church, in village on Ledbury to Ross road. *Open:* Easter Mon., Spring Bank Holiday Sun. and Mon., and Late Summer Bank Holiday Mon., 1400-1800 hrs. Every Sun. in June, July, August and September, 1400-1800 hrs.

Private Properties Open by Appointment Only

(The following properties are private residences not normally open to the public. Their owners are, however, usually happy to show visitors around provided that prior arrangements are made in writing. They are not open under any other circumstances.)

Brampton Bryan Castle. 3 miles E. of Kington on A4113. Mr Christopher C. Harley, of Brampton Bryan Hall, Bucknell, Salop, is always delighted to allow visitors to see Brampton Bryan Castle, which is in the grounds of the Hall, if application is made in writing. Brampton Bryan Hall is not open to the public at any time.
Kentchurch Court. Off B4347, 3 miles SE. of Pontrilas. *Open:* parties only, by appointment on written application to the Estate Manager.
Lucton School. On B4362, 1 mile NE. of Mortimer's Cross. *Open:* by prior arrangement with the Headmaster, Lucton School, nr Leominster.
Sufton. ½ mile N. of Mordiford, off B4224. *Open:* by prior written appointment with Maj. R. J. Hereford, Sufton, Mordiford, Hereford.

(All the above information is correct at the time of going to press.)

Appendix 2

A SHORT GLOSSARY OF ARCHITECTURAL TERMS

ARCHITRAVE: (of column) main beam, or epistyle, resting immediately on the capital, or top of column; (of door, window, arch, etc.) the surround, or moulding round the exterior.
ASHLAR: masonry which has been wrought to an even face and square edges.
BAY: the internal compartments or divisions of a building.
Each bay is divided not necessarily by walls but by supporting joists, columns, pilasters etc., in the walls.
BARGEBOARDS: projecting boards, usually decorated, in the gable of a building to hide the horizontal timbers.
BRACES: timbers which are inserted to strengthen others, usually at an angle.
BOLECTION: a moulding raised above the general plane of the framework of the door or panelling in which it is set.
BRESSUMER: form of beam used in timber-framed buildings in order to support the superstructure, which frequently projects.
CARYATID: figures, frequently female, supporting an entablature.
CHAMFER: the surface made by cutting away the square angle of a stone, or wooden block, beam, etc.
CORINTHIAN: see Order.
CRUCK; CRUCK TRUSS; CRUTCH TRUSS: an early form of roof-truss, consisting of two curved beams (locally called blades) extending the floor to the ridge.
ENTABLATURE: in Classical terms and architecture, the whole of the horizontal structure above a column (i.e. architrave, frieze, and cornice).
FINIAL: exterior beam-ending, usually carved.
FRIEZE: in Classical architecture, the middle division of a Classical entablature; in more ordinary usage, the wide band dividing wall from ceiling and frequently decorated with moulding, etc.
GAZEBO: a lookout tower, or a small raised summer-house in a garden, frequently part of a wall or placed near to it.
HA-HA: the ditch surrounding a garden and dividing it from the parkland.
HOUSE STYLES:

hall-and-cellar type: hall on first floor with rooms below usually vaulted. Found as early as 12th century.

H-*type:* hall between projecting wings. One wing usually contained the solar, or the living rooms, and the other the general offices. This was the usual type of medieval house used, with variations, down to 17th century.

L-*type:* hall and one wing, usually found in smaller houses.

E-*type:* hall with two wings and central porch. Usually 16-17th century.

half H-*type:* a variation of the *E*-type house without the middle porchway.

courtyard type: houses built around a court, sometimes with only three ranges of buildings with or without an enclosing wall and gateway on the fourth side.

central-chimney type: usually a plain rectangular plan for smaller houses only.

IONIC: see Order.
JAMB: side of doorway, window, etc.
LANCET WINDOW: small window with pointed arch.
LANTERN: a small turret, usually circular or polygonal but sometimes square, with windows all round and rising above the roof to form a cupola or dome. Usually incorporated to give light into a central, windowless portion of a house.
MULLIONS: vertical posts or uprights dividing a window into lights, usually of stone.
ORDER: in Classical architecture the Orders refer to particular styles of columns, and are divided into Doric, Ionic, and Corinthian. Each Order consists of columns with their capitals, bases, and the lintels above. The

bottom portion of this latter is called the *architravure*, the middle one the *freize*, and the projection the *cornice*. The proportions of a Classical building are all based on the diameter of the column and are thus interrelated.

OVERHANG: the projecting portion of the upper storey of a house, frequently found in timber-framed buildings.

PALLADIAN: style of architecture based on the principals of Andrea Palladio, *c.* 16th century.

PEDIMENT. the low-pitched gable used in Classical and Renaissance architecture above a portico, sometimes above doors, windows, niches, etc. When the centre portion of the base is omitted, it is termed a *Broken Pediment*; where the centre portion of the sloping sides is omitted it is called an *Open Pediment*.

PILASTER: a shallow pier or column attached to a wall.

PORTICO: the centre-piece of a house built in Classical style with columns and pediment, usually forming something in the nature of a covered porch.

QUOINS: the dressed stones at the angles of a wall.

ROOF STYLES:

single-framed: transverse rafters which are not tied together longitudinally

double-framed: rafters divided by longitudinal members such as ridge beams, purlins, etc.

hipped: a roof with sloped instead of vertical ends.

half-hipped: partly vertical and partly sloped.

belled: usually hipped but with a slight, belled curve.

tie-beam: beam connecting the two slopes of a roof across its lowest part, to tie the walls and prevent roof from spreading.

collar-beam: tie-beam which is used higher up the slope of the roof.

strut: upright timber which connects the tie-beam to the rafter above.

king-post: upright timber which connects the tie-beam and collar-beam.

queen-post: two struts placed symmetrically on a tie-beam or collar-beam.

hammer-beam: a beam projecting at right angles to carry arched braces or struts.

SCREENS PASSAGE: passage between the entrance to the kitchen and buttery, etc. and the screen behind which is the hall of the typical medieval house.

SOFFIT: underside of staircase, lintel, arch, canopy, etc.

SOLAR: the living-room of a medieval house, usually on the upper floor.

TIMBER-FRAMING: method of building where the walls are constructed of a basic timber framework, the spaces being filled in by plaster or brickwork.

LIST OF ILLUSTRATIONS

LIST OF SOURCES

J. Aubrey, *Miscellanies* (1696)

A. T. Bannister, *Herefordshire and its Place in English History*

A. T. Bannister, *Place Names in English History*

Prof. G. C. Boon, *Silchester, The Roman Town of Calleva* (Newton Abbot: David & Charles)

A. G. Bradley, *The Wye* (A. & C. Black, 1910)

W. Camden, *Britannia* [Translated and enlarged by Richard Gough] (1806)

Arthur Clark, *The Story of Monmouthshire* [2 vols] (Llandybie: Christopher Davies, 1962)

Cooke's *Visitation of Hereford 1569*

A. Dingley, *History of Herefordshire*

J. Duncombe, *Collections towards the Histories and Antiquities of the County of Hereford*

F. Edmunds, *Etymology of Names of Places in Herefordshire*

J. Ekwall (ed.), *Concise Oxford Dictionary of English Place Names* (O.U.P.)

H. L. V. Fletcher, *Herefordshire*

H. W. Howes, *History of Herefordshire*

Francis Kilvert, *Kilvert's Diary* (Jonathan Cape, 1967)

H. M. Lacey & V. E. Lacey, *The Timber-framed Buildings of Steyning (1974)*

J. Leland, *The Itinerary of John Leland the Antiquary*

Prof. J. Liversidge, *Britain in the Roman Empire*

Arthur Mee, *The King's England – Herefordshire* (Hodder & Stoughton, 1938)

Revd Michael Mountney, *The Saints of Herefordshire* (Hereford: Express Logic, 1976)

Malcolm Munthe, *Hellens, A Herefordshire Mansion*

N. Pevsner, *The Buildings of England – Herefordshire* (Penguin Press)

Revd C. T. Robinson, *A History of the Castles of Herefordshire and their Lords*

Revd C. T. Robinson, *Mansions and Manors of Herefordshire*

Royal Commission for Historic Monuments, *Herefordshire*

Preb. A. Seaton, *History of Archenfield*

Revd W. J. Smart, *Where Wye and Severn Flow*

A. Twining, *Herefordshire and its Place in English History*

Victoria Histories of the Counties of England, *Herefordshire*

Revd Hyett Warner, *Memorials of Old Herefordshire*

Revd J. W. & Revd T. W. Webb, *History of the Civil War in Herefordshire*

Woolhope Club, *The Transactions of the Woolhope Naturalists' Field Club*

INDEX

Figures in brackets refer to illustrations